INSTAGRAM
ADVERTIS

THE BEGINNERS GUIDE ON HOW TO GROW YOUR SMALL BUSINESS USING SOCIAL MEDIA INFLUENCER SECRETS TAKING ADVANTAGE OF THE POWER OF STORIES, PERSONAL BRANDING HACKS.

Table of Contents

Introduction 4

Chapter 1 What is Instagram? 12

Chapter 2 Overview of Instagram Marketing 19

Chapter 3 Choosing Your Name................................... 35

Chapter 4 Find Your Niche 47

Chapter 5 Marketing Success Within Your Reach 60

Chapter 6 Growing Your Followers on Instagram 80

Chapter 7 Determine what your Customers value 94

Chapter 8 How to Develop a Content Strategy 101

Chapter 9 How to Convert Your Followers into Buyers 114

Chapter 10 Instagram Ad Campaigns........................... 121

Chapter 11 Understanding Analytics 133

Chapter 12 How Does the Instagram Algorithm Work? 147

Chapter 13 How to Make Storytelling More Compelling by Knowing Your Audience 158

Chapter 14 Tools, Links and Resources on how to win with Instagram.. 165

Chapter 15 Different Ways to Make Money on Instagram ... 180

Conclusion 188

Introduction

In the 21st century, the interaction between brands and customers has undergone a significant change. Indeed, customers expect businesses to use visual means to communicate and it poses a whole set of challenges because they need to adopt new marketing strategies and techniques. This expectation that customers have has promoted brands to connect with their customers in new ways. In this book, you will learn different ways in which you can get more than 20,000 Instagram targeted followers and convert them into paying customers. You will learn about the best marketing tactics, Instagram ad campaigns, grow your Instagram business profile organically, email marketing tactics, about Instagram marketing funnels, and a lot of other things.

Using Instagram as a "me too" strategy is not a good idea. Businesses and brands, in their hurry to jump onto the Instagram bandwagon, don't make the necessary effort to understand and utilize the platform to its fullest. You will not be able to successfully deliver your message if you don't have any interesting content.

A lot of brands are unable to market their products using visual media because of their inability to create relevant and suitable content at the pace that Instagram dictates.

Instagram is relatively new compared to all other platforms of social media like Facebook. Instagram was launched in 2010 and has over 800 million active monthly users now and this number is growing every day. This platform is popular not just with Gen-Z users, but millennials as well. Visual content has gained a lot of traction and it is the future of marketing. If you want to use Instagram to market your brand or business, then you need to become a visual storyteller to develop an effective content strategy that will help you connect with your target audience. Instagram is a popular mobile app that enables the user to share photos and videos. A feature of Instagram that distinguishes it from other social networking sites is that it restricts photos to the shape of a Polaroid image and provides multiple filters you can apply to an image. Instagram is a social networking service for sharing photos and videos that were originally created for smartphones. Since its founding in 2010, the platform has become hugely popular, especially among millennials.

Leveraging Instagram for Business Marketing

Leveraging Instagram content for your business is actually not much different than using any typical channels that you would otherwise utilize. The same principles apply. You must be sure to know your audience and know what they are going to be attracted to. When you have done this, what will happen is your audience will naturally come your way and that will help your business grow. There are some things you can to do make it happen though, and when you effectively leverage Instagram for your business, this can lead to some incredible profitability. Here are some tips to make Instagram work effectively for you.

Consistency is a Critical Key to Success

The thing about Instagram like all social media is that consistency is vitally important. Make sure that you create a theme and that you stick with the theme. You should only post on Instagram once per day, and while business owners that do not have social media managers may find this cumbersome, if you developed the content calendar, you will have Instagram stuff locked and ready to go for the day.

Next, understand that there are two types of content – there is your personal content and your business content. If you go on a vacation and you see something on vacation that is connected to your business but would be on brand for you, post it. Of course, make sure that your followers expect it. For example, you should always post at the same time of day. So, if you like the idea of posting at noon, have things ready to go by then. Be mindful that your visuals are your brand. So, back to the vacation idea, you should not be posting photos of you in a swimsuit on the beach if your business is something that is completely unrelated – this would give your customers the impression that you are not professional.

Use Call to Action Content Every Time

Calls to action are vitally important for making sales, this means that if you are posting something and there is nothing for the person to do, then your post is not successful. For example, if you have an e-commerce store for jewelry and you are posting about your wares, the best thing to do is have a link in your bio and a call to action telling customers that they should click on your bio link above to see the piece of jewelry along with others on your e-commerce site. This is a call to action that can be put on the Instagram image or it can be embedded in the caption. Either way, a call to action is essential for any sales copy, and Instagram, although it is images, traffics in sales copy.

Have Contests on Your Instagram Feed

A great way to get people to give you their e-mail addresses and or other contact information is through a contest. Here's the thing – you may need to give away something in order to get more back in return. Let's go back to the jewelry store that was referenced above. Maybe you do a giveaway for a nice bracelet but what people need to do to get in the drawing is click on the link taking them to a landing page for them to submit their e-mail address. This is a really easy way to capture leads. The best part is people could end up browsing on the site and purchase items, or you could use that e-mail list for promotions and in turn that could result in someone coming back to your site and making a purchase. Ultimately, these contests end up paying for themselves in terms of profit margin and the little bit you needed to do in order to get the lead.

Use Instagram Stories to Breathe Life into Your Product

When people tag you with their use of your products then what you can do is repost and give them their time in the sun because they are promoting you. This will gain you lots of credibility because there is nothing more that followers enjoy like being a featured person or account of someone they are into. That being said, the Story is a great way to make this really work and then some. Encourage your followers to post Instagram stories of them with your product or talking about your service and how it has changed their lives. This is a really simple way for your followers to show how much they love what you do and a great way to connect with new customers. You can also use stories to showcase things that you are doing for customers as well. So, if you are developing a new product or service, the story is a great way to peel back the curtain and build excitement as people are gearing up for a launch day. When these stories are well done, there is a better than good chance that they will end up going viral – and that is something your business will always love.

Use the Influence of Influencers

There are many people who wish they could be Instagram influencers and then there are actual influencers. This is a network that you really want to tap into, but don't just try and get a big time celebrity or Instagram influencer to tout what you do – seek out someone who has real credibility with the audience that you are seeking or someone within your industry. This is the type of targeted influence that can help you get to the next level with your products and services. In fact, as you start working with influencers you will notice an uptick on the activity on your Instagram account. This is a simple way to appreciate everything that influencers can do for you and your business. Having influencers steer their followers towards you is a great investment as well. The best influencers know that you are willing to pay a premium, so while it is smart to develop a good relationship with them, understand they are not going to post your content for free unless it is something that can add value for them.

Any time you can provide value for these influencers, it is definitely something that you want to do. At the end of the day, Instagram influencers that do the job right are great allies to have on your behalf as you are growing your business – especially if you are a start up company.

In this book, you will learn about different ways in which you can get more than 20,000 Instagram targeted followers and convert them into paying customers. You will learn about the best marketing tactics, Instagram ad campaigns, grow your Instagram business profile organically, email marketing tactics, about Instagram marketing funnels, and a lot of other things.

So, if you are ready, then let us start without further ado.

Chapter 1 What is Instagram?

Nowadays, technology keeps on expanding and finding new and different ways to connect and help people. Thorough technological progress (iPad, Smartphone and Computer) that allows us continually connected to the whole world, a huge amount of people are on the internet every moment. Depending on where you are, a simple social media post could touch thousands of lives. Yes, technology can be scary at times, too. However, since it is the way that our world is going, we must feel comfortable using it and having it benefit us.

When I started my small business, I had trouble trying to figure out routes to advertising. Television and banner ads are often passed by and not even glanced at anymore. People know what to ignore. So, why would I want to waste my advertising budget on something that no one looks at anymore? This is when I began to consider other avenues of putting myself and business out there. One day, I was looking at my phone and saw the app for Instagram. Since I am able to use this app to post pictures on my social media pages and to other followers of the app, the idea sparked in my mind to use Instagram as a way to promote my business.

Some of you might not know or understand what Instagram is. Many people are not tech savvy, and this can affect a business. Since the world is moving towards technology, I encourage you to learn and use methods that will get your name and business out there. It might take some time and self-education, but knowing the new trends in technology can help you to become more successful in your business ventures.

Now that we have established the need for new types of advertising and why technology is a great way to promote yourself, I'm going to talk about how to promote yourself with Instagram. For those of you who don't know or understand what Instagram is, I'm going to give you some details which will help you to understand why it's a great way to promote your business.

What is Instagram and how is it Used?

Instagram is an application that can be used to take pictures and video. These pictures and videos can be posted on other social media sites, such as Facebook, Twitter, and Flickr. The photos and videos come out square, not the typical wide pictures that you are used to seeing on the computer. When filming a video, you can film for up to fifteen seconds.

The app was developed in 2010 and has steadily increased in popularity. Millions of users worldwide have the app on their smartphones and other devices. As the app developed, the developers encouraged users to use hashtags to connect with other users. This has been a widely popular way of getting pictures and videos to go viral. When something goes viral, millions of people will see it, making it a hit online. This is a great way to expose yourself to the world.

In the app itself, you use the camera on your device to take a picture or video. After the photo is taken, you have the opportunity to run it through filters to change the appearance of the picture or video. The app comes stocked with dozens of different filters, so you can alter the textures, colors, and shapes within the photo that seemed so normal just a moment ago.

After you have your photo ready to post to social media, you are able to add hashtags to the photo to describe what it is and what is going on within it.

People who are looking at these hashtags will be able to view the content that you have just uploaded.

Instagram is used by millions of people, many being in their teens to early thirties. The ability to customize your personal photos has been a huge plus to having and using this app. It can be found in the Apple Store, Google Play, and the Windows Phone Store. The app is free and can be easily downloaded and used instantly.

How is Instagram Used?

People use Instagram to share their personal videos on social media. However, that is not the only use for the app. Businesses have taken to advertising with it, and others have tried to promote their causes by using it. If you have a message to get across, then Instagram can be a tool to help you do that.

When you get ready to post your picture or video, the hashtags will guide other users to your content. Depending on the quality and catchiness of your content, it can then be shared with their friends, and their friends can continue to share it. The impact of one picture can be exponential!

Now that we have a basic understanding of Instagram, let's take a look at some creative ways that you can draw the masses to your business or cause by using this popular and well-known app! It can't hurt!

How Can Instagram Help You Develop Followers?

Having followers and customers is incredibly important when it comes to running a business or a cause. If you don't have that support, then your cause will fail. However, people struggle to get this initial following, making it difficult to stay in business. Knowing this, the first step to gaining popularity is to get yourself out there and promote your niche. It might not be an easy task to begin with, but once you have loyal followers, then you will start to see a following rise up behind it.

Instagram is a great way to gain followers. By using the features of the app, such as hashtags, you can easily send a picture or video out onto the worldwide web for millions of people to view. If you are on any form of social media, you will see posts from Instagram all the time. It's these photos and videos that can be shared and sent around the world by simply clicking a share button.

However, you need to get the hang of using this app before you can professionally use it to promote yourself. I encourage you to download it right now if you do not have it already. Take some fun pictures and videos and play with the filters on the app to see what you can do. This might give you some ideas on how you can advertise using this form of social media.

Once you know the app and its features, it's time to get serious and use it to advertise and promote. Think of ways you can capture the essence of your business or cause. This can happen in many ways. It can be through words, objects or actions. Whatever you feel will catch the feel for your business, use it in a picture or video.

Taking your pictures and videos and editing them, you might find some amazing elements that will be an even better tool to helping you gain followers. Use your time and imagination to make the pictures and videos work for you. Once you have a great post, take it to your social media page and post it with hashtags. Keep an eye on your post and see how far it can go!

You might want to try a few test runs with other topics in your life before actually putting your business out there. It will give you a good idea of how to use the app and what you can do differently to make sure that your post will get shared and spread all over. You might have to play with the app for a while in order to get the results that you want. However, having the experience and knowledge is just one great way to make your technology work for you.

After you are comfortable, you are able to register for Instagram for business. This is an area that caters to businesses and will help you to promote your business on social media. This takes a few minutes. You can create a business user name and put a tab on your social media page which will take people who visit it to your Instagram photos and videos. This is great way to get your personal friends to go to your business page and start building word of mouth.

The next part of your adventures into using Instagram to promote yourself is getting creative and getting posts out there that will bring people to you!

Chapter 2 Overview of Instagram Marketing

In social media marketing, Instagram is one of the newer tools that will help you grow your brand recognition. If your goal is to get recognized as a brand or become an online celebrity, then there is no way that you will be ignoring Instagram. Instagram will help you, as it has billions of monthly visitors. Instagram will give you the platform you need to grow and be successful, but do not take our word for it. There are many resources that can show you how many people have become celebrities. That is all thanks to Instagram, and you can genuinely grow it to a multimillion-dollar brand. There are many things Instagram can help you with; let us talk about the basics and go from there.

One of the first things Instagram can help you with is building a great SEO. If you do not know what SEO is, it means search engine optimization. If you want free, unpaid traffic, the best way to go about it is to rank high on Google. Google appreciates it when a website has a bunch of social media platforms they are connected to, more specifically, Instagram. If you have

Instagram, and you promote it, the chances are your site is going to rank extremely high on Google. Instagram will not only give you the platform to grow, but it will also give you the free and paid traffic that you have been searching for. Secondly, Instagram will help you tremendously to network with many successful businesses and people. In 2019, many people are resorting to Instagram to connect and network with people. The reason behind that is you can reach many people online; most of them will only connect with you on Instagram. If you are looking at the accounts you follow, you would know that something as big as Nike puts an effort on Instagram, and promotes their products there.

This is the reason that you must use Instagram not only to build a portfolio but also to connect with people and go from there. Many people call Instagram as an entity's online resume, so treat it as such. Another thing Instagram can help you with is to get invited to events and travel opportunities. Building upon the networking part of Instagram, many people who are active on Instagram will get invited to events where they can talk and meet with people. It will help you not only to travel the world but also to grow your business as a brand.

Finally, one thing that Instagram can help you with is advertising. Be visible to your target market online so that they can buy your products. If you are in the market of growing your business, there is no better way to reach your market than by using Instagram marketing.

You are essentially paying Instagram to target specific people, which will help you to get more sales. Primarily, every single brand on this earth uses an Instagram advertisement to get more sales. This is one of the essential things you can do to grow your business. Instagram does it all for you. It helps you connect with people. It enables you to build your brand, and finally, it helps you to be the person you want to be. There is no excuse for you not to use Instagram, whether it is for personal use or to grow a brand.

Will Instagram Work for You?

As you might know, Instagram has over billions of people visiting online. Recently bought by Facebook, Instagram has indeed grown in the past year. When it came out, it was mostly a place for people, primarily photographers, to upload their photos. Now, it is a place where you can connect and grow your brand. Many of you might be wondering, is Instagram easy to use, and can it be used by an average person who does not know how to take photos? The truth is that Instagram can be used by anyone who has a smartphone and can take a picture. This means that you do not have to be a professional photographer, which is what makes Instagram one of the best tools to follow when it comes to growing your brand and getting more recognition.

All you have to do is take a photo of your product or yourself and post it on Instagram. Your goal in posting on Instagram is to establish a call to action. Whatever you post must have a call to action. For instance, if you are posting a product that you are looking to sell, include a "Buy It Now" tagline. Or if you are trying to get more engaged followers, write down on the comments, asking what they think about this post. It is effortless to get involved followers and to get people to buy your products by simply following the rule of a call to action. All you need is an iPhone or android that can take photos for you to post on Instagram. Thanks to Instagram, you can edit it and make it even look more professional.

Your main goal should be to post relevant content two to three times a day. Think about the material that you are about to post on your Instagram. Make sure that whatever you post relates to your brand and the people you want you to follow. Do not post about cars if your page is about to makeup. Posting twice or thrice a day and keeping the content relevant will help you to keep your audience engaged. That is one of the most important things to remember when starting your Instagram and growing exponentially. The only thing you need is a smartphone that you can use to take photos. Sometimes, you can even repost other people's photos by simply tagging them in the post. This will help you to grow that brand. Also, make sure to post content about your brand. Doing so will help you grow your page even further. The truth is many people use Instagram stories to increase their engagement rates. Make sure that you leave no stone unturned and that you are genuinely engaging your audience. With your products, you need to grow it into a big brand.

Convey Your Message

One thing to remember is always to convey your message. This would mean having a call to action. For instance, let us say that you have finally completed your video or post. Make sure to ask your viewers to like it or leave a comment. This will allow you to convey your message without sounding spammy. It also makes sure that they do so at the end of your post/video.

It Has to Be Both Ways

You have to realize that social media has to be both ways; it is a relationship between the brand and the customer. Hence, having a great engagement rate is very important when it comes to building up your social media platform and brand. One thing to remember when increasing your engagement rate would be to stay connected with your fan base. Always reply to them, and be positive toward whatever they have to say. Even if they are negative, always respond in a positive manner. One of the best ways to practice 2-way communications on your social media accounts is by acknowledging the positive comments coming from your audience or followers. You can do this by commenting back with a simple "Thank you." Another way is by affirming their comments on your posts by writing things like, "We know, right?" or "Spot on!"

The most crucial two-way communication can happen when somebody posts something critical or negative about your brand on its social media account. Never react to it with the same spirit, emotion, and tone of writing in which the negative comment had been posted. Instead, take the high road by, first, acknowledging their concern, e.g., saying something like, "I am sorry to hear that" or "I can imagine why you feel that way." By responding that way, you will not be validating their critical or negative comments about your brand or post. You will just be telling them that you are not dismissing the way they feel, or you are saying that their comments are as logical as eating soil on a hot summer day.

In many cases, bashers are disarmed when they hear (or read) that their comments were not easily dismissed or when they see that their opinions were validated, even though they were not necessarily accepted to be exact or accurate. Doing so also shows your audience that your brand is classy and professional.

A basic definition of marketing is that it is an activity where products and services are promoted to prospects or potential buyers to maximize sales. So the apparent goal of marketing is to sell as many of a product or service as possible.

The 4 Ps

Marketing activities are composed of four essential elements, which are collectively known as the 4 Ps. These are the product, price, place, and promotion. To effectively sell your products and services through social media, you will first need to get a basic grasp of these four elements or 4 Ps.

Product

In the marketing industry, product refers to the process of knowing, choosing, and creating a product or service to sell. To create a product or service that will sell well, you must learn to look at your products or services from the perspective of a buyer. To be more specific, you must learn to look at three critical things: your target market's needs or wants, your products' or services' ability to meet those needs or wants, and your competitors' products and services.

Price

Price refers to the consideration you are willing to receive in exchange for your products or services. How much money you are eager to collect from your customers? This is possibly the most competitive aspect of any product or service. Competitors try to bring their prices as far down as possible in an attempt to get more customers to patronize them.

And while lowering prices is often considered an excellent competitive strategy, there will be times when raising prices may be the wise thing to do. When? The best situation where you can raise your product rates is when the competition is limited or even non-existent, and the demand for the product is very high. Another consideration is when your products or services are considered a luxury, like Rolex, Porsche, or Apple. If you are in the luxury niche, the relatively high price can even make your products and services more desirable because it will establish your customers as belonging to an exclusive or elite group who can afford such luxuries.

Oh, pricing is not just about the amount paid for your products and services. It may also include payment terms and complementary items that can increase your products' and services' perceived values. For example, a relatively high-priced item can sell many units if customers are allowed to pay for it on an installment basis.

Place

Place refers to how you will bring your products and services to where your customers are or how your buyers or clients can access them. Being an entrepreneur, it is essential for you to regularly review how your business can get your products or services to your customers. Even the cheapest of products and services will not sell much if customers can't access them.

If you are dealing with a physical product or service, location is a significant consideration. You may have to relocate your business to where your customers are. However, if you are wise enough to take advantage of social media marketing, in terms of promoting or selling your product, you can use the Internet to deliver it to your customers. Then the location will not be a limiting factor for your business.

Promotion

Promotion refers to your marketing strategies and tactics and how you implement these to make as many people aware of your products and services as possible and, more importantly, buy them. The more people are aware, the bigger your market is. The bigger your market, the higher your sales can be.

Promotion involves practically all means by which you can bring your products or services to your prospects' attention. And more than just doing that, the development also includes how to position your products and services in their minds, i.e., how they will perceive them in the best possible way. An excellent example of this is Apple's iPhones. While arguably the most expensive smartphone on the market today, it still sells a whole lot of units every time a new model comes out. People are willing to camp outside retail stores several nights ahead of the release of the latest models to make sure they are among the very first people to get them. Why? Apple, Inc. was able to position the iPhone in the minds of millions of consumers as the Mt. Everest of smartphones with a sense of exclusivity and sophistication. For instance, some claim that the

Chinese smartphone Xiao Mi churns out some of the best performing, top-quality smartphones in the world for a fraction of the price of even the lowest model iPhone. But why do people still pay more than they should get practically the same performance from an iPhone? A sense of exclusivity and sophistication would be the answer. For example, Xiao Mi's phones are highly unlikely to give the same touch of class, elegance, and exclusivity as the iPhone does, even if it comes to the point when the former might outperform the latter. But the iPhone is better positioned than any other phone in terms of quality. That is the power of positioning.

Promotion is the primary topic of this book and, in particular, social media promotion. Now, let us get into the meat of social media marketing, shall we?

Instagram is a social media platform where not only you can upload your pictures and short videos but also edit them with various filters and borders, among others. You can post on Instagram and share the same posts on four other social media platforms, including Facebook and Twitter. Many businesses have started to shift to Instagram marketing for selling their products and services simply because our minds tend to process information better through sight (visuals) and sounds. Some of the biggest names in the business that are actively marketing their brands on Instagram include Red Bull, Virgin America, Adidas, and Intel. And they do so in different ways.

Virgin America takes a less creative but practical approach to market on Instagram. An example of this is how they promoted their first-class flights. They took photos of the immensely popular Pomeranian puppy named Boo on their trips and posted them on the Virgin America Instagram account.

Others like Intel take a relatively more creative approach to Instagram marketing. They market their latest computer processors but not by showing pictures of the chips or processors themselves, which are very dull and boring to look at. Instead, they post well-edited photos of the top computers that use those processors. By showing off the sexy machines that used the boring-looking chips, Intel can engage its audiences and promote their products more effectively. They can do this by showing its audience which of the top and visually stimulating computer models their chips are being used.

The credit card company American Express also takes a creative and indirect approach to promote its credit card services through Instagram. In particular, they do not post pictures of their credit cards; that is also boring and limiting. Rather, they post pictures of the activities and events that the company sponsors. They also make use of hashtags on their Instagram posts to position their financial services as a necessary part of fulfilling and living the modern lifestyle.

While you can upload short videos on Instagram, they need to be short (maximum of 30 seconds only) in order to be meaningful. If you'd like to upload videos, better do so on YouTube instead. Instagram, for social media marketing purposes, is best suited for posting and editing great pictures.

And speaking of focusing on pictures, social media marketing on this platform is not as simple as pointing, shooting, and uploading. It is a bit more complicated than that, but not so complicated that you will not be able to do it yourself. It begins by planning your content. You have to think about your content and choose the kinds of images that you will strategically share on your brand's Instagram account.

After taking the pictures or images that you determined will be best for your social media marketing campaign, you will need to edit them to give them the "oomph" or "wow" factor. You can edit them using the app itself right before you post them. Instagram features several cool preset filters, or you can customize them yourself using the app if you are familiar with photo editing. Doing this can turn "ok" into "great" and "ho-hum" into "wow"!

Lastly, you can optimize your image's contribution to your brand's overall social media campaign by coming up with perfect hashtags. Doing so can help the leading search engines easily categorize your pictures into specific keyword categories and make them even easier to be discovered by others.

Other Instagram Best Practices

One specific way to do this on Instagram is to post images or pictures of the people who make up your brand or products and services. And that includes posting pictures of you! Doing so will give your brand a "human" face and something to personally connect to.

And when people see the faces behind the brand or product, they are more likely to trust it, engage with it, and patronize it.

Another way to help your prospects and existing customers connect with your brand on a deeper level is to post images and pictures of the behind-the-scenes stuff, such as how your products are made and packaged or how it looks like when you render the service you are marketing. Posting pics and images of things like these can help people trust your brand better due to a better sense of familiarity. They know what goes into your products, who the people rendering your services are, etc. Just be careful not to show too much information on the posts so that your competitors will not be able to copy you.

Chapter 3 Choosing Your Name

The first thing that you are going to have to do is set up your Instagram account. If you already have one, then you do not have to worry about this because you already have an account and so you already had your username in place. What you are going to need to do is build your profile so you will have to put your full name, your username, password, and a photo. Now, remember what you are going to put your username as is how people are going to find you. The name that you choose for your Instagram page is going to be vital. Your Instagram name is going to be what people use to see you so think about it as a website. There are thousands of websites on the internet but you have your favorites that stick outright? They have done something to make you recognize them and not other people. When people search for you, it is your name that is going to need to be recognizable and it is going to need to be something that pops right away. The way that you are making your name is going to be what determines a significant amount of your success on Instagram. Chances are that you are not already a famous celebrity that everybody knows or a famous company and brand that is monetized all over the world that everybody knows. The chances are you are just someone who is just starting out and you want people to notice you and notice your brand. Therefore, what you need to do is maximize your growth on Instagram and the first way to do that is to choose the right name.

Remember that people will be disappointed if they cannot see content that matches your name or they are going to be confused because they are not going to see the correlation between the two. A great example of what we mean here is if you are a vegan. If you are a vegan and you are posting content about eating cheeseburgers or eating a steak, this is going to make your followers not like you because they're going to see that not only are you not doing what your name implies but you're going completely against what your name implies. Another way that this will confuse your fans is they would think 'why are you eating meat if you are a vegan'? This is a very simple and a bit of an obvious example but it can really help you see what we mean. Another example that we could state is if you are a woman who claims that she will never wear luxury items and you are spotted with a Gucci handbag your fans will know you lied. This is not what they want. They want someone who is real and not pretending. There are a lot of fake profiles on social media already. Focus on being real and true to yourself instead. Things like that are really, what is going to make a difference. It sounds like common sense but many people will just jump into this process before they think about it and then it is harder for them to get started.

Here is a trick to consider. There are over seven hundred million people that use Instagram and chances are, your name is already taken. So let us work around it. This is what we mean. Think of keywords like inspiration, or wanderer, traveler, and things that are like that. If you use the words alone, they are taken. If you try to use them together such as inspirational wanderer, or travel inspiration, things that are like that will give you a better chance to make sure that it is not taken. Choosing two complementary 'buzz' words gives you a much higher chance of finding something that has not been taken, but you still have the chance to have SEO optimization. SEO means search engine optimization and what this means is that when you type a word into Google, it will find you simply and easily and you appear at the top of the list instead of on-page five or six of the results.

Think about the content you are going to post and have your name have to do with that content. Like we said above the name and content need to go together well and not be confusing but to be concise and clear so that you do not confuse your fans and followers. A great way to help you decide on your name is to write a list of buzzwords that have to do with the type of content you will be posting. Let us say that you are going to have a bookstagram. For this, you will want to write words that have to do with books. Such as the following examples.

- Library

- Reading

- Books

- Fantasy

- Romance

See these little buzz words would show up really well on a Google search. This is what is going to help you get seen and found. Make a list of about ten or fifteen words. Then you can choose. You can also choose alliteration and this is a great thing to use for your name as well. Let us say that your name is Tony and you want you are wanting your account to be about traveling and seeing the world and beautiful sights. You could name yourself TravelingTamy. The alliteration is clear and concise which means it is easy to find you and it is easy to say. If you choose not to do this that is fine too. Another tip is to try an adjective with the buzzword. For this example, we are going to take you back to the book lover. So let us say that you are a fan of the old-time libraries and the beauty of what they can create. A house for thousands of stories and pages for you to learn and explore.

You can use some great adjectives here to make that name stand out. Think carefully about some great adjectives here. You could name yourself moving library since you are traveling to different places to find them each time, you could go with walking library to give the illusion that they move around as you do, there are many different things that you could go with here to make your name stand out so strongly that no one will be able to forget it.

Choosing a surprise word to make yourself seen can work great for you as well. Think about your niche and use words that would go with that. When you think of traveling, you might not be thinking about seasons but this could be a cool idea to get you noticed. You can call yourself the seasonal traveler or something that has to do with that title or you could think about the word barefoot. In today's society, the word barefoot means that your free and your moving and making sure that your ability to be in a sense or have any sort of idea about oneness with yourself. When you are traveling, you can make this work for you. You could say something like a barefoot traveler, or barefoot wanderer, there are many different ways you can go with this and make your name be better.

Originality is important because it is going to make a huge difference on your account and you need to avoid a brand name in your name as well particularly if you are not a member of that brand. If you want to look like your part of a community or brand, make your own brand and remember that brand names can get lost in the crowd. Rhyming can help you get into the right mode as well because they are funny while being cute and fun and they can really help you get noticed and bring people to you.

Other easy tips that can help with your name are to add I am in front of it so that they know it's the real you and so that you can let them know that your the one they are trying to find. Another great thing you can do is get your account verified although this is something that most celebrities do because they are more well known than others are.

Instagram has a checker to see what is available and what is not and there is no limit to how many times you can try. Get creative and use what feels good to you and your heart. If all else doesn't work and you end up choosing a name that you later hate, you can fix this and change the name without losing the followers you already have but it can cause issues for those that want to follow you. Particularly if you have chosen to connect all of your accounts or you have the same username on your other accounts. You will have to change all of them if you do this and some do not give you the option to do that.

If you are still having issues with coming up with a name for yourself you can be frustrated and this an issue with you. This is not an easy thing to do because it is a complicated thing for a lot of people and that is alright. If this is true for you, you can use what is known as a name generator. There are plenty of online tools that you can use for free. You will be able to use these to help you come up with ideas for a name for yourself. The only thing that you will have to do is plug in a few keywords and it will give your ideas for what you should do for your name.

This next tip is actually kind of fun and you will be able to think of something unique. Think of celebrity couples. You play with their names and give them a cute name as a couple, right? Think of Ben and Jennifer. They began to call them Bennifer. This is a combo of their names. The same thing with a famous model that was on a famous show. Her name was Melissa Rose and she shortened it to Melrose. In a later season on the show, one of the models said they respected her idea and did the same. She shortened her name from Whitney Michelle to Whittelle. You can do this with your name too! Let us say your name is Christine Lewis. Put it together and your username can be Crewis. Interesting and fun, it would not be the sort of thing you would see every day. Another trick with your name is to rearrange your name. This is different than what we have just said above. Think about it like this. If your last name is

Stan, you could change the letters around and play with it to find something you like. Maybe you could change it to tans or another word from the four letters.

You can also reference your location for something that is a little different, you can remember that your name can have to go with what your brand is, and you can use clues and words that tie into your personal brand and what you are trying to achieve. You can also use your title. Think about a famous doctor or celebrities. They have a title that sets them apart and it helps people find them and recognize them so that they can have more people know who they are.

Look up keywords to try to find something that appeals to you and what you are trying to achieve. If you notice that the keywords your typing in have a lot of results and followers, you've just walked into a highly competitive field. Just remember that you need to be creative. Remember also, to keep it simple. Instagram gives you thirty characters for your username. Nevertheless, that does not mean that you should pack it full of symbols, letters and other things because it is going to be an overly complicated potential mess.

Take your time to get a nice name. Ask people you trust because they are going, to be honest with you and there are other things that you need to consider as well like pronunciation. Let the name be easy and unique. The shorter the name the better.

Symbols. Do not utilize two or more periods or symbols in the same name or right beside each other. It becomes hard to search and find the name. You should also keep ethnicity and religion along with other things like gender out of the name as well. Your name should contain relevance to what you are posting.

Using your niche as a keyword in the first section of the name can help as well. Enter the client's mind – get to know how they are searching for your related niche and what first thing do they type for searching. That keyword. If it is not, then your name could get lost among the other search results. This is a really simple way to utilize search engine optimization within the app. Avoid popular names and huge Instagram accounts. Another great tip is to make sure that your name is on different social media platforms and while we mention this above there is another thing to think about when doing this. Therefore, what we mean is if you choose a name on your Instagram and you have that name on your other accounts as well, this is going to ensure that your brand is simplified and unified. The only exception to this would be if you wanted to keep your personal account separate from the account to use for business and influencing. Obviously if you don't want people to find your family or your friends and you want to keep your personal life separate, then you could create a different account with that same name for your fans to see and they wouldn't be able to see your family or friends and this is okay because many people want to keep their private life private. With the issues going on in today's society that's honestly a very good idea to keep your private life private and separate because this eliminates the potential chance of stalkers and other problems.

If you have a website then you should have the name be very similar to your Instagram name. You do not need to spend a lot of money to make your own website and honestly, if you are just starting out a website might not be the best option for you because it takes a lot of time. However, if you are going to go this route because of the opportunities that a website will afford you then make sure the names are similar so that they can find you easier or make them exactly the same if the website allows you to do this. In certain cases, they do not allow you to do this so just be aware that that might be an issue.

By understanding the tips that we have given you in this chapter you should be able to come up with a name for your Instagram account that will be engaging, fresh and cool while making sure that you have the option to be unique and you will be able to gain followers. Once you gain those followers, you will be able to let you keep those followers because they will be able to find you through the keywords that you have used. You will also be able to take your Instagram to the next level, which is what we are trying to achieve here. The name is the first thing and now that we have covered it, we will be showing you how to find your best niche. This is a very important part of Instagram and as such, we will be giving you all the information about your niche and how to choose the best one possible for you.

Chapter 4 Find Your Niche

A niche market is a small and specialized chunk of a larger, more general market which, in turn, comes with a specific selection of product interests and customer demographics. To illustrate, consider the market for online dating which can then further be broken down into things such as sacred sexuality, green dating, polyamory, soulmates and more and each of these can then be further broken down into sub-categories such as soulmates over the age of 40 and gay green dating. In a world where every niche is already accounted for, sub-niches are a great place to start, though not every sub-niche is automatically going to be profitable which is where doing the right research comes into play.

When it comes to starting down the path to social media marketing, it is important to approach the process with the idea of forming a brand around the thoughts and opinions you currently hold or are interested in learning more about. Once upon a time, you could have a site that functioned purely as an aggregate of a specific affiliate marketer's products but any more, that type of site will be removed from Google search results as it does little to add new value to the Internet. This means that you will need to be marketing yourself as much as the products in question when it comes to finding success in the pay per sale or pay per lead world.

This means that when finding the right niche of products to market you need to consider more than just what the most profitable products are but also what are the ones you can put your name behind and build a brand around. One of the most common ways of doing so is by becoming an authority on the niche in question by doing lots and lots of research and then sharing that research with the appropriate types of links filtered in. Depending on the affiliate marketing potential of your hobbies, those are always a great place to start, but there are other ways to find the niche that is right for you as well.

If you find it difficult to come up with any potentially profitable niches right off the bat, then odds are you are not looking at the world around you through the eyes of a social media marketer. To do so, simply make it a point to go about your daily grind, taking notes on all of the actions you take and the conversations you have as well as anything you hear or read about. At the end of the day, all you need to do is to then sit down and find two potential niches related to every topic that you have written down. They won't all be winners, and many of them might not even be profitable, but the exercise should be enough to get the juices flowing and reveal great niche potential that was hiding in plain sight.

Another great place to find inspiration is on the longest running affiliate programs by far, Amazon.com. If you visit the site and then click on the search tab you will be given a list of all of the different types of items being sold, all of which have potential niches associated with them. What' s more, clicking on each of these options will bring up an even more specialized list of options, which, again, all have niches and sub-niches associated with them as well. After you find a few items, you can simply work backwards and determine the niche that would be interested in the items in question.

Narrow down a niche

Find a target: The first thing you will want to do when it comes time to find the right niche or sub-niche to call your own is determine who it is you are going to be targeting directly. There are several different ways you can determine your target audience, the first being the audience that you yourself are a part of. Alternatively, you can choose an audience that you have similar interests with.

If you can't seem to find an audience that speaks to you, you can instead find a niche that speaks to you and determine the audience you are going for from there. Regardless, it is important to find your audience and speak to them directly as, for example, you will find that a 25-year-old male student has very different needs, wants, and interests than a middle-aged female professional.

Consider the problems: The next thing you will want to do is take the time to really consider your target audience, or, failing that, yourself and think about any desires, aspirations, pain points, challenges, and problems that you or the group in question might have that they are going to regularly be looking to mitigate. A good way to determine if you are on the right track is if a simple Google search for the problem in question reveals plenty of blogs, websites, and forums discussing it. A problem isn't really a problem if no one is talking about how to solve it.

Find the profit: Once you have found a few problems that people are looking to solve, your next step will be to determine which are the most profitable from a marketing sense. You will want to go to Adwords.Google.com and look for the keyword planner tool. This will let you filter search results to find just those you are interested in before searching for local and global results. You will want to find the monthly searches for the topics in question, the number of searches resulting from people trying to solve the problem in question, how long those terms have been returning the results in question and how readily information about that topic already is.

Additionally, you will want to do basic searches related to the niche and make sure there are plenty of advertisers already taking advantage of the customer base. If you are having a hard time finding pages with actual advertisers, you may need to ask yourself what products you are going to actually be marketing. Taking the time to stop and think about whose products you are going to advertise at this point can be a huge resource saver in the long run and is highly recommended.

Dig deeper: In addition to understanding that a particular problem is often had by a specific group of individuals, it is important that you understand exactly what this group wants when it comes to solving a problem, for example, if you are targeting individuals looking for soulmates, you need to understand both what that means to them, how they approach love and what specifically they are looking for in a soulmate.

This portion of the process is all about going as deep as you can to learn the thought processes of the group in question but also the type of specific slang, lingo, and the language they use to describe their desires in relation to your niche. The more you know about your market, the more you can use that knowledge to create the type of ad copy and sales pitch that speaks to them specifically.

Decide if you are willing to go the distance: Once you find a niche or sub-niche that you like the look of, it is important to determine what type of content your target audience is looking for and decide if you have the ability to provide the level of quality that they are looking for. This means going the distance with the products you are endorsing every single time, and really immersing yourself in the relevant culture.

While investing in a few items that you plan on marketing might seem like a major step, the best affiliate marketers are those that create a compelling story around the items in question, and physically having the item in front of you goes a long way towards building that story. Additionally, you will want to spend the resources to acquire a high-quality digital camera and the expertise to use it properly. This doesn't mean every potential customer is looking for art in every photograph, but it does mean they are looking for quality shots, nevertheless.

Determine the number of merchants: While even the least active sub-niche imaginable has at least a few merchants who cater to it, those who are looking to build their first niche marketing site should start out in a market with a bit more variety. Your goal for multiple affiliate programs to already be in place, which will ideally allow you to set up multiple compatible compensation agreements per site.

Consider industry trends: In addition to determining the number of merchants working in the space in question, it is important to determine if the market in question has already peaked, and if so, how far in the past that peak actually was. You can use the Google tool for determining trends for this exercise and it is a great way to easily determine if a particular niche is on the way to a popularity explosion or if it went bust years before you ever started thinking about affiliate marketing. In scenarios where the biggest spike appears to have already happened, but it did so recently, then the niche in question might still have potential. Major peaks that were several years ago without a repeat performance should be avoided as a general rule.

Determine if there is a way in: In highly competitive niches there are likely a handful of websites that make up the first page of the Google search results which makes it practically impossible for anyone else to break in on the SEO front. If this is the case with a niche or sub-niche that you are considering you will want to see if there are other available avenues outside of the more traditional routes.

Prove to yourself that you have ideas for content: When it comes to deciding if you have what it takes to create a new social media marketing plan around a specific niche, it is important that you take the time to outline around 50 ideas of major content that can easily be tweaked once your pages launch. This should be different from the day to day posts that you will be generating to keep a steady flow of new commission opportunities and should be the potential types of high traffic posts that will generate new repeat visitors. This is the content that will put your site's best foot forward and you should plan on posting about 3 per week. If you can come up with 50 ideas, then several months from now you might find yourself running out of ideas.

Consider what the competition is doing: Knowing your competition and siphoning their audience is another common tactic available on Instagram. When you go to your competition's page, you can view their followers. From there, you can engage with their audience by following, liking, or commenting on their followers' posts. According to studies done by Shopify, following will produce a 14 percent follow back rate. A follow combined with a like will increase that number to 22 percent, and a follow + like + comment will garner a 34 percent follow back.

Of course, you can always expand beyond your competition's list. Browse hashtags and other popular users or photos. Put thought behind which photos you choose to like and make comments on. If you were viewing an Instagram photo and the last comment was interesting, chances are you would likely check out that account, right? Another tip to this method is to try and be the last person to comment on the photo. Utilize your emojis when appropriate and be unique.

Profitable niches to think about

If, after going through the steps above, you still haven't found the right niche, some of these evergreen options might be just the thing to set you on the road to long term affiliate marketing success.

Romance, wealth and health: When it comes to social media marketing, health, wealth and romance niches, and sub-niches are thought to be infinitely profitable because new products are always coming along for all three and the customers for each are always likely to be looking for the Next Big Thing.

- The health market includes things like medical issues, smoking cessation aids, embarrassing issues, and weight loss trends.

- The wealth market includes things like business opportunities, multilevel marketing, affiliate marketing, gambling, forex, and internet marketing

- The romance market includes things like finding a spouse, reconnecting with an ex, pick up tricks, attraction tips, and online dating.

Each of these evergreen markets has countless niches and sub-niches housed within it and countless potential customers who have already been groomed to expect a new and improved way to solve their perceived problems on a regular interval. This means there are people out there right now that are waiting for you to tell them while some new product will solve all of their problems when used properly and will be back again next week looking for something new as well.

Expensive Hobbies: Alternatively, while you yourself might not have a hobby that can be easily monetized in an affiliate marketing sense, that doesn't mean that there aren't plenty of hobbies out there with plenty of digital and physical products for the marketing. When it comes to choosing the right hobby, consider the types of things that those with lots of disposable income like to spend their time on.

Depending on the market in question, you may be able to contact merchants directly and arrange for personal demonstrations to give your content a unique touch. These types of niches are also great because there will constantly be a new stream of gear and digital products and there is also automatic content for holiday posting as a gift guide with links isn't just appreciated, it's expected.

Merchants known to pay well: While the types of niches that fall into the big payout category are typically quite competitive, that doesn't mean there isn't always going to be room for the right new person on the scene. High payout merchants include travel companies, jewelers, designer handbags, luxury watch, online casinos, a luxury boat, and car rentals as well as payday loan companies. The idea here is that it takes the same general amount of effort to generate positive advertising content for a $10 item as a $100,000 one, which in some cases may actually be true.

These types of business all tend to be recession-proof as the luxury items are targeted at those for whom money is no object, payday loans are always going to be right for someone, and gamblers are always going to need a place to gamble which online casinos are happy to provide. Again, these are not new markets which means that the competition will be fierce, if you enter into the prospect with a clear idea of just what is going to be expected, however, there is no reason you cannot find the success you seek.

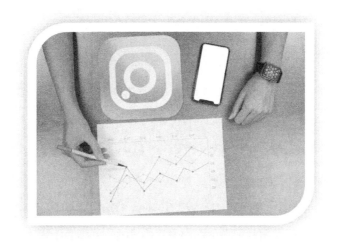

Chapter 5 Marketing Success Within Your Reach

Powerful marketing campaigns can do wonders to transform the performance of your business. From struggling to make a sale to going viral in a day, anything is possible when your marketing campaigns are powerful enough to leave an impression on your customers. Optimizing your marketing campaigns for Instagram should be the core focus of every campaign you intend to run, and there's a lot of work that goes into creating just one campaign alone.

Time, effort, commitment, and not to mention, the budget that is spent, crafting a campaign to perfection until its ready to launch means you need to make sure all your bases are covered. This isn't as easy as it sounds, though, especially when your ideas and ambitions don't line up with the marketing budget you have to work with. Even with a limited budget, though, it's still possible to create powerful campaigns. A great campaign doesn't necessarily have to be accompanied by a big budget all the time. It is still possible to do when you know how to work Instagram's advertising tools to your advantage.

How to Create Powerful Campaigns

Creating powerful ad campaigns without having to break the bank requires careful planning and strategy. Plan your most powerful campaign using the guidelines below as a reference:

Step 1: Start with Your BEST Objective - Your objectives list would probably have a few items on it, and it can be hard to narrow it down to just one. Every objective feels like it matters (and it does), but a powerful campaign requires focus. To do that, you need to pick the BEST objective out of that list and focus on that. Otherwise, you're going to end up with an ad that is trying to do too much at once, and at the end of the day, it ends up not being very effective at all. It is always trial and error though when you're attempting to set up new ads, especially in the beginning, so don't get too frustrated and allow yourself some time to adjust to the process and get the feel of how things work best.

Step 2: Every Campaign Has a Name - Every campaign you plan should have its own name.

Naming your ad is like a tracking system which is going to keep you organized, and it helps you keep track of what works and what did not. You can pick your campaign names based on campaign type, country, network, demographics, language, and basically anything that you'd like. That way, when you need to refer to a successful past campaign while planning your future ones, recollection is a lot easier and more detailed when you can quickly refer to *Campaign A* instead of trying to randomly recall bits and pieces.

Step 3: Deciding on Your Ad Placements - Instagram's Ad Manager feature provides you with a few ad placement options to choose from. You want to familiarize yourself with their options *before* you start selecting your target audience because it is going to help you decide if this ad is going to actually work well on Instagram, or if it would be best on another social media platform altogether. Ad placements must be edited according to the social media platform because it allows you to better track the performance of the ad. Your Instagram ad campaign should be optimized for the ad specific to the platform, avoid using a standardized format across all your social media profiles. A placement which works well on Instagram might not perform as well on Facebook or Twitter, for example, and vice versa.

Step 4: Zone in On Your Audience - Save yourself a lot of time and money by targeting the right audience group from the very beginning. Your target audience is going to be the tipping point of your campaign, the one that determines if it is a success or failure. To fine-tune your audience reach, select them based on age, gender, location, language, demographics, behavior, and connections to name just a few. By zooming in on the details and fine-tuning your reach, you'll save yourself from spending precious dollars out of your already limited budget targeting the wrong group of customers who aren't going to yield any tangible results. Once you have selected the right audience group for your ad, you'll see the option of "Audience Definition" on your ads manager display. Use this function, because it is going to tell you if you have targeted your audience too broadly or too specifically.

Step 5: Customize Your Budget - The great thing about Instagram is the flexibility it offers when you need it. Like when it comes to budgeting, for example, which is completely customizable based on your needs. Since Instagram's advertising runs on the same platform as Facebook ads manager, what happens with the daily budget is that Facebook will spend a fixed or designated amount to help you deliver your ads each day on the campaign dates that you selected. The lifetime budget option lets you choose the amount you would be willing to spend during the dates of your ad campaign. Once you've chosen your budget, you will then select the schedule for which your ad will run. This will depend on the timeframe which you have set when you were planning the campaign in the initial stages. It is recommended that you choose the option on Instagram that states *run my ad continuously starting today* if you are looking to build brand awareness.

Step 6: Ad Format Selection - Once you're done setting your budget, schedule and deciding on who your target audience is, the next step of the process is to choose the Instagram ad format that you are going to go with. If you're on a tight budget, you're going to want to take your time carefully selecting the best ad format, so you get the most out of it. Different ad formats will produce different results, and with Instagram, the six different types of ad formats that you get to choose from are Carousel Ads, Single Image Ads, Single Video Ads, Slideshow, Instagram Stories Single Video, and Instagram Stories Single Image.

Step 7: Launch Campaigns with A Cause - Customers want to see that a brand is more than just focused on making sales and profits. They want to see that your brand cares about something other than its sales figures. A campaign that showcases your brand caring for a cause is a good way to shine the spotlight on your business. Your campaign for a cause should be a cause that your audiences will be able to relate to, something that resonates with them. For example, Dove launched its #DoveWithoutCruelty campaign, which emphasized the brand's commitment to not test its products on animals. Dove partnered with PETA and other social media influencers to promote this cause and it resonated well with a lot of other Instagrammers out there.

Maximizing Your Marketing Campaign Potential

Instagram has made it easier than ever for businesses to sell their products and services on social media. Social media marketing today is not an option anymore. It's a *necessity.* Conventional advertising methods are slowly on their way out. If you want your business to get noticed, you need to be on social media. It's safe to say that every second you're not on social media is another second which is wasted because you could have been improving your brand awareness and driving sales.

Consumers these days prefer online shopping more than any other shopping method. The convenience that comes with online shopping is a huge incentive, and when these consumers are easily able to reach out and contact the brand, that motivates them even more because of the customer service experience that they receive. Powerful marketing campaigns help nudge your consumers in the direction to take action. While there may not be any sure-fire guarantees, what you can guarantee is that if you do the best that you can to ensure you're maximizing your campaign's potential, you stand a good chance of coming out on top.

Be Short, Move Fast - Social media is a fast-moving platform, and Instagram is no different. Customers spend only seconds on an image or video before losing interest and moving onto the next. They come here for the visuals and the videos, and they *don't* want to do a lot of reading. Keep your content to a maximum of 40 characters and nothing more, Instagram is the ideal example of a platform where less is more, in this case, especially when it comes to texts and words.

The Power Lies in Your Visuals - Not just images, but high-quality video content, too. Fantastic photos are what Instagram is all about. If you want to bring in the sales, boost your brand's reputation, and grab the attention of new customers, high-quality images need to be your no-break rule for every piece of content you produce with each marketing campaign. Customers these days are not about the hard sell anymore; they want something that is genuine and authentic to look at.

Don't Overshadow Your Product - A good rule of thumb to follow is that your branding should not be overshadowing your product. If it is, then you probably need to scale back on the branding a little bit. While you do need to feature your brand and logo on every content your produce, you may need to do it in a subtle manner so it doesn't appear like a "direct sales pitch" or hard sell.

Working Landing Pages - Customers will be extremely put off when they arrive at your landing page only to run into technical issues. All that hard work you put into your campaign is going to be futile if your landing page falls short since the customer won't be able to complete the final purchase anyway. Always test to make sure your landing pages are in working order so no one is left disappointed at the end of the day.

Testing 1, 2, 3... - Run a couple of "test ads" on your Instagram stories and profile to see how your audience responds to it. Do they like your content enough to engage with it? Or is it not getting the response that you hope for at all? If it is the latter, it might be worth reconsidering if you'll want to spend money on this campaign. Test runs are a good indicator of whether your full-fledged campaign is going to work the way that you intend it to, which could end up saving you wasted money.

Never Forget Your Call-to-Action - The whole reason you're running this advertising campaign in the first place is because you want to see some real sales results. Without proper call-to-action, your customers are not going to know what needs to be done next. A call-to-action prompts and reminds them what the "next step" should be. *Shop now, sign up now, apply now, contact us now, watch now, and download now* are some examples of a call-to-action you should be using, depending on the nature of your campaign.

Common Marketing Mistakes

Instagram, in many ways, is a great platform for businesses to share their creativity while building a connection and a lasting relationship with their customers. For the inexperienced marketer though, there's a lot of potentials for risky mistakes to be made. Even experienced marketers could fall prey to social media marketing faux pas on Instagram that could kill the sales of your business. Some mistakes on social media could end up becoming costly affairs, bringing all that success and momentum you've built to a halt if you're not careful.

While sometimes mistakes do happen despite your best efforts, it's still best to avoid them altogether if you can. Mistakes can be learning opportunities, but sometimes, those lessons could cost you more than you bargained for. Where possible, you want to minimize the mistakes to maximize the potential. Let's look at some of the common marketing pitfalls that get made on Instagram:

Mistake #1: Buying Followers - As thrilling as it is to see your Instagram following quickly climb to an impressive count, you're setting yourself up for trouble if you give in to temptation and start buying followers. This isn't just a mistake, it's almost like committing fraud. Fake followers have become such a serious thing that brands have started adding it to their contracts drawn up with influencers. Not only do you run the risk of harming the reputation of your brand by discrediting it, but there are also real legal consequences which you might have to contend with. Since these followers are fake, your return on investment is still going to underperform anyway, since no real sales can be made. Customers might not trust your credibility again, and for a business, this is a very serious issue indeed.

Mistake #2: A Lack of Engagement - Avoid treating Instagram as merely a platform for you to sell your content because that's not all that it is, and treating it as such is only going to lose you followers in the long run. Failing to engage enough with your customers is another mistake that a lot of marketers tend to make. Customers expect you to be responsive to their queries or comments, and the quicker you are to reply, the happier they will be. If all you do is sell, sell, sell, and ignore them, it won't be long before they turn away from you and head right to your competitors.

Mistake #3: Only Relying on Images - It may be an image-centric platform, but with the other available ad options which have been introduced, there is no reason for businesses to just stick to one source of promoting their content. Customers are going to be bored very quickly with monotony. Avoid limiting your advertising potential to just one content source and don't be afraid to experiment and play around with the other options.

Mistake #4: You're Rushing - Getting so caught up in just trying to dole out content regularly to remain active on Instagram that you forget or overlook the quality aspect of it all is another frequent mistake that gets made. This mistake can pose a challenge because, on the one hand, you need fresh content daily so your customers don't forget you exist. But on the other hand, trying to come up with ideas for quality content every day is not such an easy task either. Every now and then, you will experience the occasional mental block and be completely stuck for ideas on what to do next. The stress of publishing daily could cause a lot of businesses to rush and post less than perfect material. Forgetting a call-to-action, missing some hashtags, and a description that doesn't quite match your content are some examples of what could go wrong when you rush before you're ready.

Mistake #5: Inconsistent Frequency - If you post too much, you run the risk of spamming your customer's newsfeed. But then again, if there's too big a gap between your last post, you're at risk of appearing like an inconsistent or inactive business profile. You don't want to be one of those businesses that post a ridiculous amount of content until your customers get tired of it, but neither do you want your postings to be so sparse your customers wonder if you're even active on social media anymore. It's a fine line to balance, but it is a great example of why you should never ignore your analytics. The less information you have to work with, the more susceptible you will be to committing errors.

Mistake #6: Forgetting Your Captions - An oversight that a lot of marketers end up making when they think Instagram is all about the visuals. That captions are secondary and don't matter as much. Captions may not be as long or descriptive as they are on Facebook or other social media platforms, but they still *do matter*. A well-composed caption has always been a crucial part of starting conversations on social media. You need great captions to cement the point that you're trying to make, and without them, your visuals simply may not be powerful enough to tell the story that you want to be heard.

Mistake #7: No Concrete Goals to Guide You - It cannot be emphasized enough how important goals are to success. Every campaign that you plan *must have goals*, you simply cannot achieve the level of success you want without setting a goal that is going to point you in the right direction. Without setting proper goals, you leave your campaign open and vulnerable to mistakes getting made more frequently than ever. Remember how having no goals is like shooting in the dark and hoping you'll get lucky? This can turn out to be a very costly mistake when you're ill-equipped to deal with the challenges that are going to come along the way when running your ad campaign. If you aren't clear about what the aim of your ad is, you'll never know if what you're doing is working or not.

Best Instagram Marketing Tips

We've become so used to seeing ads on our newsfeed these days that it feels like they have been around forever. Each day, as you scroll through any of your social media platforms (not just Instagram alone), within a minute or two, you're bound to encounter an ad. Maybe even within seconds of scrolling through your newsfeed, that's how common they have become. They may have been around for some time now, but businesses are still figuring it out, experimenting to see what works best, trying different tools and tactics as they get a feel for the feature, and determining what's going to work best for their business. There's always something new to be learned and discovered, as these social media platforms themselves continuously work to improve.

One of the reasons why navigating social media platforms is an ongoing learning process is because not every platform works in the same way. They each come with their own set of strengths, advantages, all of which can be used to help benefit a business's overall campaign goals. Instagram is no different. Being a platform which is all about the visuals, Instagram is unique because it offers advertisers an outlet for them to get inspired. To discover new, creative possibilities and to bring those discoveries to their brand as they continue working diligently to enhance the experience of their audience and customers. Being an image-focused (and now video too) platform, first and foremost, Instagram hasn't lost its touch and stays true to that concept even through their ad offerings. They know it's because this is what the viewers have come to expect, what they have become accustomed to.

To get the most out of your marketing efforts on this platform, you need to position yourself one step ahead of your customer. Anticipate their needs, figure out what they want even *before* they do. Managing a social media marketing campaign is hard work, but there are certain tips and tricks you could take your profile, marketing, and advertising efforts from good to better, and finally, to *exceptional.*

- ***Tip #1 - All Your Liked Photos In One Place***. Did you know that there's a quick way to view all the posts you've liked on Instagram in one place? Go to the "Options" tab, and then click on the "Posts You've Liked" selection. If you want to unlike any of them, just tap on the image and unlike the content. Don't worry, the user won't be notified that you've stopped liking their content.

- ***Tip #2 - Saving What You Love.*** View all your most-loved content and save them for easy viewing later on by simply bookmarking them. On your profile, you will notice that there is a bookmark icon at the top-right above your images. Tap on it, and select the "Collections" tab. If you haven't created one yet, simply select the "Create Collection" and start saving all your favorite content.

- *Tip #3 - The H.D.D (Hide, Disable, Delete)* - Good business practice would be to *not* disable comments on your profile because this is one of your means of communication with your audience and customer base. However, if you do have to hide it, delete it, or even disable commenting for any reason, here's what you would need to do. Head on over to your "Options" tab once more, and then select on "Comments". Once you've done that, you'll have the option of filtering through your comments based on the keywords. Try toggling "Hide Inappropriate Comments" and key in the specific keywords which you're after so you can keep an eye out for comments that may not be the best fit for your profile. To delete comments, you'll need to head over to the speech bubble icon, which is located below the comment that you're looking to delete. You will then need to swipe to the left. There'll be a "trash can" icon that appears after you do this, and by tapping on that, your comment will be gone. If you're wondering whether you can disable comments entirely across your profile, the answer is no. Unfortunately, disabling needs to be done for each individual post. If you've got a post you don't want people commenting on, use the "Advanced Settings" option before you post your content. Choose the "Turn Off Commenting" option and no one will be able to post any comments on that particular post.

- ***Tip #5 - That Extra Special Font.*** There are always ways to make your profile stand out, one of which is by using special fonts. Ordinary keyboard typing limits your creativity because there's only one option to go with - whatever the keyboard presents you with. As always, third-party solution providers come to the rescue, and all you need to do is head over to these websites and copy special fonts from there. These fonts are not often found with Instagram and its community, so when you utilize these fonts, your profile will really stand out and be memorable. Websites like Instagram Fonts and LingoJam are a good place to start.

- ***Tip #6 - Stay "Fresh" Without Deleting.*** Delete all your old, outdated content *without actually removing any* of them from your profile. This keeps your profile looking fresh, updated, and always on-trend, the way your customers expect it to. Head to the post which you want to "remove" and then tap on the three dots at the top of the post. Next, select the "Archive" option to archive the content. You can review your archived content anytime by selecting the "Archive" icon, which is located at the top right corner of your profile page.

Chapter 6 Growing Your Followers on Instagram

The more followers you have, the higher the chances of you engaging with users and offering them unique experiences. However, growing the number of your followers is not an easy feat, and many brands try to take the easy route. They do this by paying for likes or followers on the tons of websites offering these services. But the truth is, if you want to get the best results for your brand, you will have to grow your audience organically.

According to statistics, over 40 million users on Instagram are fake! Amazing, right? However, ever since this statistic initially became popular, Instagram has been making lots of efforts to clamp down on counterfeit followers permanently. In fact, it has gotten rid of over 700 million fake accounts over the years!

What this means is that, regardless of the number of followers you currently have on your profile, if they are not genuine, they are not heading to your landing page or store. Also, it means they are not telling others about your website or the services you render, nor are they buying anything you sell. This is an important reason for you to pay attention to growing an organic and genuine audience on your Instagram page, or any other social media platform, for that matter.

You may understand this, but it may still seem like a better option to buy followers, right? After all, all you have to do is pay, sit back, and watch your follower count grow. For this reason, we will be taking a look at some of the benefits you stand to gain from increasing your followers the right way.

Why Do You Need to Grow Your Followers Organically?

Here are some of the reasons you need to grow your followers the right way on Instagram:

Access to More Features

Features like Instagram stories are great for sharing the story of your brand. The story feature has been observed to amass a higher level of engagement in comparison to other formats. Besides, the stories feature can be a massive source of revenue and traffic. Using this feature, you can share a link to other websites on Instagram. The other site in this instance could be your store, and it is made possible using swipe-ups. This is the only other location you can share links aside from your bio which lets you share a link.

But, if you plan on using the swipe-up link feature, you need two things. One is to get your page verified, which is not exactly an easy thing to do. The other is to have no less than 10,000 followers. So, in essence, when you grow your followers, you get access to this feature, which will help bring in more sales.

More Followers Translates to Enhanced Reach

Instagram is a platform that remains organic. Even though there are solutions that require payment, it is still possible for you to engage and reach a sizable number of your audience without the need to invest any cash whatsoever.

For this reason, the more people following your page, the more the possibility of them coming across your content and engaging with it. Also, using a well-planned-out hashtag strategy will ensure you get great results.

More Followers Means More Credibility

You may not like it, but the fact is that having lots of followers on Instagram translates to credibility. It is the same way influencers operate. If you are offering great content consistently, lots of people will engage your content, like and share it. In doing so, a higher number of individuals will do the same, and so on. The number of people following your account has a way of influencing any choice not to follow or follow you. This is the reason so many marketers are tempted to pay for follows - the credibility factor.

Having a high number of followers goes beyond a wow factor, it is critical. The reason is that the organic reach you possess and your capacity to produce actual results in your marketing efforts are all dependent on leveraging the number of individuals who follow your page on Instagram.

Knowing this, the next step you need to take is to learn the strategies that can help enhance your number of followers. There are lots of ways you can increase your following on Instagram going forward without using a budget, and we will be taking a look at some of the top ones below.

Ensure Your Account Is Optimized

The very first and easiest step in growing your Instagram followers is to optimize your account. Like we have covered earlier, this has to do with creating a great bio and profile. If there is no profile image, username, or bio, people will not know your brand owns a specific account. This may not seem important, but lots of brands fail to add a link on their bio to a landing page, while some even fail to fill it in the first place. This is your number one location for driving traffic from Instagram to your website, so it is vital to take all the steps in fully optimizing your account.

If you are not sure about where to link, you can leverage product or marketing pages which have to do with specific campaigns, hashtags, and keywords on your account on Instagram. It is fine to link your homepage, but you can also ensure users get a cohesive experience when heading from your bio to the website of your choosing.

Also, remember to ensure your username is easy to search for. If your brand has a lengthy name, you can make it shorter but still relevant, so your audience will have no difficulty in recognizing it. Stay away from unique characters or numbers when creating your username as it makes it more difficult to understand.

Post Content in A Consistent Manner

The biggest mistake you can make in your bid to get Instagram followers is to post content irregularly. If you can get followers by chance at the start, the last mistake you want to make is to stop doing the things that made them follow you in the first place.

A great way of dealing with this is to ensure your posting schedule is consistent. Typically, brands should not post more than a few times each day. However, regardless of the route you choose to take, make sure it stays consistent. More than 200 million users on Instagram check out the website each day, so to spread your reach more, you can spread your posts all through the day.

By adopting a schedule and sticking to it, you will be able to develop a consistent experience for your followers.

Create a Schedule for Your Posts Beforehand

Even though there has been a change in the Instagram algorithm to allow users to view more of the content they are interested in, posting at the appropriate moments still ensures your posts have higher visibility.

There are many tools you can use to easily schedule content for your Instagram profile in advance. When you do this, every member of your team will be able to see schedules and campaigns more effectively. It is a wise decision to plan your content using scheduling tools, as they can let you reach your target audience and also maintain a consistent content flow. A few tools that can help with scheduling include Later and Hootsuite, among others.

Encourage Other Accounts to Post Your Content

An excellent method of making sure more users follow you is to be present and get your brand into the feeds of your clients. You need to do this on other Instagram pages in addition to your own. An easy way to get into the feeds of your customers is to sponsor UGC (user generated content). Also, you can run contests on Instagram to ensure your brand reaches a broader audience.

An equally great technique is to let your username reach a broader audience. You can do this by collaborating with more established accounts in your field and getting them to share your content with their followers. The great news is that you can go beyond Instagram to do this. All you need to do is ensure that your content offers value to the audience. Collaborate with other brands to develop your audience on Instagram.

Besides this, you can capitalize on your other social media platforms like Twitter if you have more followers there.

Learn How to Tell Real Followers from Fake Ones

Like we covered earlier, there is a difference between an account on Instagram with fake followers and one with authentic ones. It may seem less challenging to buy Instagram followers, however, the downsides outnumber the benefits.

Fake followers on Instagram:

• Mislead New Followers: If lots of new users follow an Instagram account with tons of followers, but later find out there is nothing of benefit being offered by the account, they may feel deceived and unfollow your account anyway. It is not ideal for deceive users into following your account. A better route would be to develop long-lasting relationships and trust to get enhanced engagements.

• Do Not Offer Any ROI: Even though purchasing followers is very easy, the followers you purchase will not buy anything you are selling or visit your landing page in the first place. Users follow Instagram brands because they like the brand or what they are posting. These users are the type that offer real cash value to brands.

• Don't Engage: If you have 100,000 fake followers, they won't comment, share, or like any of your content. These accounts may later get deleted by Instagram, leaving your posts without any form of engagement.

Authentic followers can like, engage, share, and leave comments on your Instagram posts. These users also love it when there is an individual leaving responses or engaging with them. In turn, you get to have more individuals following your page, which in turn grows your follower count.

Promote Your Instagram Page

If you fail to promote your Instagram page, it won't be possible for anyone to find your account. To do this, ensure you link your Instagram account with your other social networks and website.

One of the top ways of ensuring users discover you is to develop awareness and visibility. If your goal is to increase the number of followers on your Instagram page, it is important for you to let them know where they can find you. If you own a blog or website, you could incorporate social media buttons to any of them as this will help encourage users to share your content and let them know where to locate you on Instagram.

Another fantastic technique is to promote your Instagram account on all your other social media accounts. It is possible to capitalize on your other networks on social media to direct visitors to your Instagram page. However, make sure that you are not only requesting for people to follow you. Instead, make efforts to share fresh content on your Instagram page to give users a reason to follow you.

Post Content Your Audience Desires

This may not be easy to achieve. However, it is a wise choice to learn the types of content your followers would love to see. You will easily observe that there are a few types of content which do better than others on Instagram. This is the reason why it is important to experiment.

Regardless of if it is your post time, captions, filters or types of content, the littlest detail can make a huge impact. Watch out for recent trends on Instagram so you can be sure you are posting content that is trending at that moment. To make this less complicated, you can capitalize on Instagram analytics tools as they will make it less difficult to analyze and track Instagram content.

If you are not sure about where to begin in regards to your content strategy, you can check out what your competitors are doing. However, it is not advisable to just copy what they do. Instead, take a look at the way they post, pick ideas, and improve upon those ideas. This can set you ahead of the game. With what you learn from your competitors on Instagram, you will quickly see what is providing results for brands in the same sector as you.

Get the Discussion Started

Starting discussions is a great way to announce your presence to users on Instagram. In a quarterly report released by social media analysis company Sprout Social, over 35 percent of customers used social media to contact customer service in the second quarter of 2016. This means that social media outranked email, live chat, and in-store customer care. This implies that the number one customer reference for businesses is social media. To boost your sales and the integrity of your brand, your company should be communicative and supportive on Instagram.

Responding to comments and questions could be vital in securing a new follower or customer. It is equally necessary for improving brand image and relationships with your followers. Ensure that interactions grow around your feed so that you can gain more followers. It has long been established that trending on social media drastically increases a brand's outreach and base.

Ensure Your Users Participate

Getting users to partake is an indispensable marketing tool on Instagram, especially if you desire more followers. But first, you need to bring in something of value. You need to be valuable to your audience, whether by promoting users on a business account, insights on the latest deals, or providing quality visual content.

User-generated content is one method businesses are using to encourage users to partake. This form of audience promotion can spur people to share content across many accounts and cause you to trend using your branded hashtags. This sort of outreach is just about what your business needs in gaining more followers on Instagram.

Find High-Converting Hashtags

It has been established before now that hashtags are one of the best means of getting Instagram followers. Hashtags assist in reaching a broader audience in social media. Hashtags provide precisely what a marketer wants: building your online community by getting more followers.

Highlighting your social media content in a pool of billions of videos and pictures isn't always easy. Hashtags have to include keywords: words or tags that members of your target group are likely to search or look up. These people will most likely follow your account, should a relevant connection e established. M&M, for instance, does excellent in localizing hashtags when they are participating in an event. The company targets its audience by making use of hashtags like #mmspotlight. This goes to create awareness about the spotlight event.

In the same vein, knowing how your branded hashtags work on Instagram is second only to using them. There are several hashtag analytics tools that you can use in understanding how they perform. One such hashtag analytics tool is Sprout Social. You have unlimited analytics as to the performance of your hashtags to get informed about what works best for your brand.

Ensure You Make Your Followers Happy

A happy customer is a returning customer. This also implies to your Instagram followers. When you make it your goal to put a happy face on your followers, you increase your audience growth rate.

These crucial tips will assist you in extending your social reach, increasing the visibility of your content, and building you a loyal audience.

Chapter 7 Determine what your Customers value

If you want to have success on Instagram, your content needs to be of exceptional quality; this is not up for debate. Your posts need to be better than your competition, much better. If you want to attract new users and peek their engagement continuously, you must provide them with content they value.

Value is a word that is thrown around the marketing industry very often, albeit is generally misunderstood. From a high-level perspective, it is easily defined: your audience attributes a level of importance, worth and usefulness to your content. However, it can be extremely difficult to define exactly what your audience value about your content and your posts, especially in the digital media industry.

For instance, cat memes are extremely popular across the web, but can you describe why people value or enjoy in these memes? They are not high-quality pictures; they are not revolutionary, are they original? Do people enjoy these memes because they can relate to the everyday problems they portray? Do users find these memes funny because they convey a message through the personification of an unlikely and cute pet in original and unexpected ways? If your Instagram page is about cat memes, you must ask yourself questions like this, brainstorm and really think about what your audience values.

Determining exactly what your users/customers value is one of the most difficult aspects of the marketing industry. However, this is also the most critical task: discover exactly what your audience demand is and only then you will be able to satisfy a market need, thus attracting new users and skyrocketing their level of user engagement.

By now, you should have developed a fundamental understanding of your target audience. You should have developed an appreciation for features such as age range, daily lifestyle/habits, social media habits and gender distribution of your followers. Use this understanding to help you understand what they value, what the market demand is and what they are searching for.

To develop an understanding of exactly what your audience values, you can follow the approach presented below:

Step 1 - Assess competition - first draft of Market needs & value proposition

When starting off a new Instagram page, as with any business for that matter, the first approach I always recommend is assessing your competition. Earlier in the guide, I described the importance of having a competition, it proves your market has an audience, user engagement and has a following.

Look at small and large competitors within your field; the smaller pages are your immediate competition and the larger pages are your long-term competition.

Look at 5 small and 5 large pages in your field; for each, write down:

• 3 aspects of their profile you like (i.e. they are funny, high-quality photos, they are relatable, they show behind the scenes photos...)

• 3 aspects of their profile you do not like. For each of these points write down how you might fix this problem, it does not have to be a perfect solution. It is an initial through-provoking exercise to develop your critical thinking and market analysis skills.

- 3 aspects of their profile you think the users enjoy: this is their value proposition. Why are users following this page? What do you think engages them? Why are they interested in their posts?

After carrying out this procedure for ten competitors, you will have developed an in-depth understanding for the market you are in and the condition of your competition. Finally, summarize in ten simple statements what people liked most about the profiles and what you could have improved. Think critically: "why were people following these pages?", "what were they trying to get out of it?". Look at the comments on their posts, analyze the people's response and feedback. The summary of what aspects of their content was well accepted by the market will serve as the foundation of your profile's value proposition. Remember: Steal the positives from your competition, learn from their mistakes.

Step 2 - Refine & improve your value proposition list

During the previous step you developed a concise list describing why, in your opinion, users are attracted to your competitors. However, copying the competition has never led anyone to success, you must improve on it. You must differentiate yourself and, in order to steal market share, you must provide content of better value.

To accomplish this object, you must refine the audience requirement list under two factors.

Step 1 – Reference your value proposition points against the target audience profile you developed earlier. Can any of these aspects be optimized to the age range, habits, gender of your target audience?

Step 2 - Play to your strengths. Do you or your team possess any unique skills you can exploit? For instance, are you an excellent web developer, an outstanding Photoshop user, an incredible video editor or a wizard at mixing soundtracks? Definitely bring these factors into your page to set yourself from your competition and provide your audience with unique content only you can provide.

Step 3 - Produce content. Following your value proposition, which you adapted in step 2 above, produce and launch content to your new page (more information on doing this effectively in later chapters).

Step 4 - Evaluate Feedback, improve and start again. As with any new business venture in life you will encounter criticism. A large portion of people decide to blindly ignore all criticism and carry on their own path convinced they know better; this is clearly the wrong approach. You will receive a lot of feedback from your audience in the form of comments, messages and likes. You must assess a portion of this feedback and reject the remaining portion. Look for constructive criticism, focus on it and try to isolate what the users are telling you, what they like and what they would like to see. If some photos have 1000 likes and other photos have 50 likes, analyze the differences between them and critically deduce what your users are looking for.

You must try and isolate why your audience responds positively to some photos. Once you have an initial theory, you must test the market! Post a new photo that addresses all of the customer feedback and examine the new response. Again, you will face positive and negative feedback; examine the new feedback, evaluate where you improved and try to improve again. This is a process of continuous improvement and is what will ultimately lead to market share domination. It is a lot of constant work, but ultimately leads to success.

Remember: great content is a prerequisite for Instagram success, one of the many factors that must come into perfect place. Having exceptional quality will not give you Instagram success—marketing, advertising, consistency, engaging followers, patience and more advanced strategies are also required.

Chapter 8 How to Develop a Content Strategy

This chapter will cover the broad aspects of your content strategy on Instagram: what you should be doing with your feed, what you definitely should not be doing, and what types of content have been successful on Instagram in the past.

What You Should Be Do

The key to doing this is to remain active. Setting up a schedule for your content and stick with it.

The top brands on Instagram post around 6 times per week. That adds up to more than 300 posts per year, which sounds very exhausting. However, frequent and high-quality posts are essential to maintaining visibility and engagement.

For people to discover your feed, it needs to have visibility. This means, if you do not have an active following yet, you need to be posting new and interesting content with regularity. Your older posts will not stay relevant in your follower's feeds, and will certainly not show up in the hashtag feeds that you need to be in if you want to grow your following.

Furthermore, posting content regularly is essential if you want to maintain your existing following. It's definitely true that most users don't clean out their subscriptions that often, but when they do, you surely want to be remembered as an important part of your follower's daily feed. Maintaining a regular schedule of content keeps your followers engaged, and therefore, they're more likely to remain your followers in the future.

Aside from this, make sure you keep all of your information in your bio and links up to date. Don't forget to update your information if you change your website, corporate identity, or location. Putting out inaccurate information is a surefire way to lose current and potential followers.

Things You Should Not Be Doing

While it is important to remain active with your account, it is equally important not to be too active. People on Instagram are looking for genuine, authentic content that they will not find on other social media platforms like Facebook. Do not treat Instagram like just another marketing platform. If you are only posting pictures of your product, people will be turned off and will not become followers.

Instead, you should post honest, interesting things that attract attention without being obvious advertisements. If you want to post pictures of a new product, tease it, don't show the whole thing. Give tidbits using interesting framing to build curiosity and engagement. The Instagram audience primarily consists of a young lot that wants quirky, interesting content that they can engage with.

Posting too frequently can also spam your follower's feed with content. And when you forcibly occupy too much of your follower's feeds with low quality, obvious marketing content, there is a high risk of being unfollowed.

You should also focus on not getting discouraged. Do not expect to get a million followers overnight. Building a network takes time and luck. If you stick to your account and develop high-quality posts, eventually you will have a breakthrough. Furthermore, do not allow negative feedback to discourage you. While Instagram does have auto-moderation features, they will not catch every inappropriate or unfortunate comment on your posts. Take criticism constructively, do not allow it to tear down your work. Instead, use it to improve your future posts. At the same time, recognize that not all forms of criticism are valid.

Developing Content Pillars

In making your long-term plan for Instagram success, you should decide on a number of 'content pillars' that will make up a majority of your posts on the platform. To start with, you should probably decide on three or four pillars to start building your brand. Pillars are the foundation of your brand on Instagram, the things people expect to see from you in their feed.

Your goal should be to develop a consistent identity for your profile on Instagram. Focus on what you want people to think about when they hear your brand name, and how you can build that image in their minds. When planning content pillars, you should focus on a consistent brand image while maintaining sufficient variety to maintain interest without diluting that brand identity.

Going through that section to identify relevant posts that are suited to your marketing goals and use that as a foundation for your initial content pillars.

Of course, even though this is how you are starting out, you do not need to restrict yourself. As you build your following, you'll be able to identify what works for your audience and what does not. Plus, your marketing goals may change over time which means you might have to adopt a new strategy. So, don't be afraid to change your strategy in the long run.

Scheduling Content

Part of maintaining a regular content schedule is to maintain a content calendar. Make a regular schedule for what type of posts your audience would like. Throw in some variety and don't repeat the same kind of posts every week. If you have a regular feature that routinely generates high engagement, schedule it more often and set a particular day or time for it so that your followers know more about your routine.

Having a schedule ahead of time can also reduce the burden of keeping up with your feed. You can 'pre-bake' a number of posts ahead of time. That is, set up a number of potential posts in a single session, then release them according to your schedule. If you have a reserve of pre-baked content, this can allow you to keep up with your scheduled content even if unexpected events prevent you from creating new content on the fly.

When it comes to scheduling content, you should be aware of optimal posting timings. Statistics have shown in the past that the highest engagement on Instagram posts are on Monday and Thursday between 8 AM and 9 AM Eastern Standard Time. In general, Monday and Thursday are high engagement times of the week outside of the 3 PM to 4 PM window, though any work-day outside of normal office hours tends to result in higher post engagement than during work hours or weekends.

You should keep these timings in mind when planning your content schedule, along with the time zone you are targeting. If you are planning for a nationwide American reach, Eastern Standard is ideal, while if your scope is more local, you should target the same time window within your local time zone.

A Few Examples of Successful Post Types

Now, we are about to cover a number of successful content examples that can be used as the foundation for your content pillars. This list is not intended to be exhaustive and we acknowledge that you might have a super great idea that no one may have executed before. However, if you're taking baby steps in the world of Instagram marketing, some of these options are a good way to start.

Behind the Scenes

One great way to use the distinctive aspects of Instagram is to post great 'behind the scenes' images, videos, and stories. The goal of this type of content is to give your followers a more intimate look into how your business operates and what it represents when compared with more sterile, traditional marketing materials.

Highlight the way your team goes about its daily routine, the process of putting your product or service together, the fun moments that emerge in breaks. Consider creating a 'day-in-the-life' through the 'stories' function. Showing your followers how the sausage is made, so to speak, will make them feel like you are giving them inside information that is otherwise inaccessible. This feeling of exclusivity can generate further interest and boost engagement.

Employee Reposts

Keep track of whether your team members have Instagram accounts, and engage with them directly if they do. Follow your team members on the platform and encourage them to follow you. Keep an eye out for high quality or potentially high engagement content posted by your employees.

Adding content to your feed this way has several benefits. First, if you have creative and energetic employees who naturally create high-quality social media posts on their own, reposting and commenting on their content is a much hassle-free way to add more content to your own feed. This content will feel 'authentic' as it was not created as a part of an active marketing campaign.

Second, engaging with your employees directly can build engagement and community within your organization, with potential ancillary benefits for morale. Finally, involving your team members in your social media outreach can convert them into ambassadors for your brand, even if marketing isn't part of their day-to-day responsibilities.

Follower Reposts

Building engagement with your followers is not a one-way street. If you want people to engage with you, you need to engage with them. Keep track of your mentions and the use of hashtags through your notifications and Instagram analytics.

Reply to their comments, like positive comments, comment or like on reposts, etcetera. If your followers know that you are watching, they are more likely to engage with you in the future.

Educational Posts

Many successful Instagram brands use educational materials as a major content pillar. Your followers are more likely to engage with content that will benefit them.

'Educational' content can take a lot of different forms. If your business is food related, it could be a recipe, tips on how to get that same great taste, or how to use your product in a familiar or creative dish. If your product is more technical, you could post detailed 'how to use it' posts and provide a breakdown of useful features. However, educational posts do not need to be directly related to your specific goods or services. You can post informative content about the marketplace or news that influence your field of business-like statistics, poll results, profit figures, and so forth. Educational content can generate high engagement because it includes a 'call to action.' If you have posted a recipe or a how-to guide, it gives your followers clear instructions on how to use your products. This produces high engagement because it encourages your followers to make you a part of their lives outside of just watching your feed.

Educational content can also be an avenue for people to discover your feed, especially if you are posting facts and statistics about your field of business. While Instagram is certainly not a primary source for people doing research online, people may still search for facts and figures about things related to your business or see the facts and figures you've posted in a hashtag feed and want to learn more.

'Piggybacking' on Influencers

Follow influencers on Instagram who interact with your business space. If you own a restaurant, follow famous chefs and their businesses. If you sell sporting goods, follow athletes. If you are a photographer, follow famous photographers and outlets that highlight high-quality photography like National Geographic. If your account is all about fashion, follow prominent labels and high influence fashion profiles. Keep an eye on what high influence accounts are posting. Interacting with a high influence account is one of the easiest ways to expose your handle to people who aren't following you yet. Repost content from high influence feeds that you follow. Comment on their high-quality posts. Highlight any example of an influencer mentioning or using your product or service. Even if they neglect to mention it themselves. By inserting yourself into the feeds of high exposure accounts that are related to what you do, you increase the chances of your handle being noticed by potential followers who are already interested in things related to your business line.

'Piggybacking' on News, Trends, or Events

Keep an eye on the calendar for current events. Watch the 'top posts' feed through Instagram's discover function to identify high engagement and trending hashtags. You should keep an eye out for hot trends, news events, or holiday that relates to your business line. There is a holiday for just about everything these days. Make a list of holidays that are relevant to your business and make sure you post about them. If a trend or news event is closely related to what you do, do not miss an opportunity to point it out. Trends can tell you what people are thinking about. If you can jump on a trend, it will increase chances of visibility, boost engagement with potential followers, allowing you to earn a couple of new followers.

Fun Stuff

Posting fun content, like 'boomerang' animations, memes, and funny behind-the-scenes moments is a great way to make your posts stand out.

Business Culture Posts

One reason you may be on Instagram is to highlight your business culture. If you have a slogan or a distinctive business philosophy, you should highlight it. The standard format for something like this would be a solid color or otherwise simple background with high contrast block text over the top, similar to the formatting for 'meme' posts.

'Take-overs'

One common strategy for high-engagement stories content is a 'take-over.' In general, this means handing over control of your Instagram account to somebody other than your dedicated social media specialist for a set period of time. Typically, you would want this person to create a series of posts through the temporary 'stories' feature.

You could do an employee take-over as a more extensive form of behind-the-scenes content. In other words, 'see what Martha from sales does in a day of work.' You could do a follower take-over, in which one of your followers showcases how they use your product throughout a typical day. Like reposting content from employees or followers, this is a low-effort way of creating highly authentic, engaging content. Obviously, you want to be careful with this type of post, and you should only give temporary control of a social media account to a trusted employee or follower who you are confident will represent the brand well.

Chapter 9 How to Convert Your Followers into Buyers

Instagram has been a boon for a lot of different brands. It is a self-promotion safe space that allows a lot of companies to showcase their services and products in a way that hasn't been done on other platforms. But since this platform is going to be limited to mostly video sharing and pictures, without help from a click through e-commerce feature, the return on investment can be a bit harder.

While we have spent some time in this guidebook taking a look at how you can build up your list of followers and get more eyes on your products, it is now time to take this a bit further and explore how you are able to take these followers and turn them into some of your paying customers.

First off, realize that not all of your followers are going to become your customers. Some people may like looking at your products or hearing news about you, but they may not make any purchases. Others may be frequent shoppers with you. And others will shop on occasion or just once. But your goal is to turn as many of those followers into customers as possible. The good news is there are a few steps that you can take in order to make this happen and they include the following:

Make all of your followers on Instagram feel like they are in your inner circle

Even on social media, people want to feel included. One of the best ways to make the person feel like they are a part of your community, and therefore make them more willing to purchase from you, is to ensure that they feel like they are actually a part of your inner circle.

It is pretty common knowledge that a bit of incentive can go a long way when it comes to seeing a boost in your sales. And when it comes to gaining some traction on your social media platform, this is still true. In one study that was done in 2013, it was discovered that about 49 percent of Americans liked a Facebook page for some company or another because of loyalty. And then 43 percent would become a fan of a certain page in order to get special deals or coupons.

The trick to making this one work is to find the sweet spot between those consumers who may just decide to follow you in the hope of getting a discount, and try to get them to stick around because they actually do like and support the products you sell. This is where your followers on Instagram are going to come in. These particular followers already have an interest in the products and brand you are presenting, but now you need to provide some incentive to get them to purchase from you.

One way that you can do this is to do a tease for an exclusive offer on the Instagram feed, one that the followers aren't going to be able to get in stores or online. This means that the special is only available to those who follow you on Instagram. This makes the followers feel special, and they may be willing to make a purchase, even if they hadn't been considering it before.

Not only is this strategy going to be a good one to drive some sales, but it ensures that the followers feel like they are on the inside. This proves valuable because they will have more goodwill for your brand. When you use your Instagram business account as real estate for your promotions, it is easier to remind your followers to start shopping now, and that they should check back often to find more steals and deals as well.

Add in a call to actions to your posts and stories

Never do a post without some kind of call to action. This needs to be on your posts and on your stories. Your followers need to know what they should do next, and as we talked about, asking them is going to be more efficient than just assuming they know what you want them to do. This call to action can get rid of any confusion and will make it more likely that you get the sale.

When you work on a call to action, it isn't always going to be a call for the customer to purchase something. Maybe it asks them to like your page, use a hashtag, or even share or repost the thing you put up. But if you have an item that you are posting about and you want to sell, then your call to action must be about purchasing that item if you want to turn at least some of your followers into customers.

Turn the store into a hot spot

Thanks to some of the filter effects and features that come with Instagram, but this platform has a way to turn almost any picture and any item that you are promoting look pretty enviable. You have probably scrolled through the feed at least a little bit and wished that you had some of the items that were there. If you are promoting your own business on Instagram, why not make sure that all the pictures you are posting of your store have that same feel.

Many brands that happen to manage pop-up shops find that they are pretty good at promoting in-store events on their Instagram pages. For example, the online retailer that is known as Piperlime is constantly showing pictures of the yummy treats that they sell and they use imaging that shows off some of their pop up parties in order to get customers more interested as well.

Instagram is working on a buy now feature

One new feature that Instagram is releasing is the purchase or buy now feature. This works similar to what is found on Pinterest and other social media sites, and it is going to lead to more followers deciding to click on the link and make a purchase as well.

Let's say that you are a store that sells shoes. You may have a sale on a pair of boots and you decide to list them on your past to promote the sale. With this new feature, you can add in a button that allows your followers to click on the link and purchase those boots. This takes some of the work out of your followers having to search for your link. And when the customer is able to click on the link right away, they are more likely to give in to impulse shopping and this leads to a sale for you.

Pay attention to the lead your fans have

Chances are that your products are out on Instagram, even if you don't have an account. This can happen when you have customers who are snap happy and excited about the products that you provide. The good news is that you can leverage some of the legwork that your customers already did and then use that work on your brands' page. This can save you time, shows off a positive review that you got from a customer, and can enhance the product because you provide a visual example of how to enjoy and use your product.

For example, on the Instagram of Ben and Jerry's, you will notice that most of the posts are going to be credited user pictures (remember to credit the follower or user when you repost their picture). Your mouth is going to water from all the good looking treats, but this profile basically just reposted pictures of their customers enjoying the snack.

When other customers get a chance to see that the product is popular, can actually see the product, and then get a chance to see how that product should be used, it can actually make the product seem more appealing. This is where that unique hashtag can come in handy as well. You can ask your customers to use that hashtag any time they post a picture of them using or wearing your product. You simply have to search that hashtag, then repost, and you have a lot of your work done for you, and a simple way to turn some of your followers into customers in the future.

The overall goal of collecting as many followers as possible is to turn them into customers. It doesn't do you much good to have 10,000 followers on your business page if none of them ever actually purchase some of the products that you are selling. When you use some of the suggestions in this section, you will find that it is easier to take those followers and convince them to purchase your product.

Chapter 10 Instagram Ad Campaigns

Successfully creating and launching an ad campaign on Instagram might sound a little scary. It is quite easy if you know what you need to do. In this section, you will learn about the different things that you need to do to attain this objective.

Step One: Research

The first step is to find the inspiration for your Instagram ads by analyzing the things that others in your niche or your industry are doing. Before you create an ad campaign, you need to check what your competitors are doing. You need to spend some time researching the kind of ads they are running, the call-to-actions they use, and the engagement they are able to get.

One of the easiest ways to do this research is to view your competitor's Instagram handle and go through their mobile website. Now, you need to go through their product page and check the specific products. If that specific Instagram account uses Facebook pixel for remarketing, then once you return to your Instagram page, you will start to see their ads on your feed along with the products you searched for. Remarketing is a strategy that targets users with specific ads related to the products they searched for previously. If you repeat these steps with different competitors, it will give you an idea about the type of ads they are running. Also, it is a great way to find some inspiration and ideas to design your own campaign.

Step Two: Campaign Objective

Before we delve into how Instagram ad works, you will need to establish a campaign objective. A campaign objective states the purpose the ads serve, and it essentially dictates what you want viewers to do when they see your ads on Instagram. There are different campaign objectives that Instagram offers, and it is given in the form of a pre-made list. The objective that you choose from this list helps optimize the ads and determines how you pay for the same. For instance, if your aim is to gain more followers, then the click-through on the ads will not be your primary priority. The different campaign objectives that you can choose on Instagram are as follows:

Brand awareness helps you reach the audience who are likely to pay attention to your ads and increases the overall awareness of your business.

Reach - Select this objective to increase the reach of your ads.

Traffic - It is ideal to opt for this objective to increase the drive the traffic to your website or the app store (if you have an app).

App installs - Directing traffic to the app store so that they can install or purchase your app.

Engagement – Engagement is important to increase the number of people who see and engage with your page or posts. It includes comments, shares, likes and, responses you receive.

Video views - As the name suggests, it is to promote the number of views the videos you post garner.

Conversion - To convert your audience into paying customers or to make any other similar valuable action.

If your marketing objective is to sell products or to run a remarketing campaign, then it is a good idea to install Facebook pixel. It is a small code that you can place on your business website to track the visitors and any other conversions. When you use Facebook pixel, whenever someone clicks on the Instagram ad, they visit the website and make a purchase, and the pixel shows a conversion. Then this conversion is matched against all those who click on your Instagram ad to see the sales or conversions you have made with a specific ad.

Step Three: Targeting

Instagram ad targeting helps you find the best audience to whom you can advertise a specific ad to. It helps you target those who are likely to perform or take the action that you mentioned in your campaign objective. For instance, if your business sells quirky socks, you will obviously want to target all those people who are likely to make a purchase. It's a great thing that Instagram ads have similar targeting options Facebook ads. You have different targeting options like location, demographics, behavior, interests, and much more.

At the primary level, your campaign needs a specific geographical region (country), gender (if it is a gender-specific product or service) and ideal age group. For instance, you can have a campaign that targets men and women between the ages of 18 to 40 who live in metropolitan cities. Try to be as specific with this as possible while you are targeting your audience. The greater the reach of the targeting ads, the better your chances of attaining conversions or obtaining your campaign goal.

Instagram also offers the option of creating custom audiences to reach all those who have interacted with your business in the past or with similar businesses.

Step Four: Creative

The fourth step is to build your Instagram ads creative. This is partially a science and an art in itself. Before you start, you need to think about your objective, the audience you are reaching and the kind of message you must deliver to encourage your audience to engage with the ad. Instagram offers different types of ad formats to choose from and they are photo, carousel, slideshow, and video ads.

Photo ads

You can use these ads to tell the story of your brand and feature different products by using visual imagery that's engaging. If you are just getting started with using ads on Instagram, then this is the safest and the easiest option to start with. Not only are they easy to set up but are easy to run as well.

Carousel ads

If you want to strategically showcase various products or multiple uses of a given product, then opt for this ad format. This format of ad allows the user to swipe to see more images and includes a call-to-action button that will direct them to a landing page to learn more. For instance, a restaurant can use this type of ads to showcase all the different ingredients used to prepare a tasty meal. Once the viewer swipes through all the images, you can use a call-to-action button that will direct users to a reservation page or something similar.

Video ads

A video ad can last for up to 60 seconds. Ensure that your ad is great and that you use the first 30 seconds wisely. This is the time frame within which users will want to engage with the business. When you are designing these ads, you need to create content that integrates well into your follower's feed.

Slideshow ads

You can create a simple video ad using a series of stills. This is a good type of ad, if you don't want to spend a lot of time creating video content for your business.

Businesses also tend to use user-generated content. If you want to promote a product using ads on Instagram, try to include some real-life situations or testimonials that your audience can relate to.

Step Five: Create the Ad

Now, it is time to create your Instagram ad and here are the steps that you need to follow.

The first thing that you need to do is link the Instagram account to your Facebook page. Go to the Settings option on your Facebook page and select the "Instagram Ads" option from the menu. Then, you need to click on "add" to get started and you will need to enter your Instagram login details to get started.

The next step is to open the Facebook Ads Manager and click on the "+Create Campaign" option in the top-left corner of the screen. You need to select the campaign objective in this step.

Once you select an objective, you need to create your Ad Set. You can define your target audience and set your budget in this step. While selecting your budget- there are two options to choose from. The options are daily budget and a lifetime budget. The daily budget option allows you to run the ad throughout the day, meaning that Instagram's algorithm will automatically pace your spending in a given day. The lifetime budget option specifies the time for which you want to run the ad for. This option will pace your spending budget throughout the duration or lifetime of the ad. It is a good idea to start with a small ad budget and you can expand if the ad performs well.

Once you set your budget, you need to select the number of images you wish to use and choose an ad format accordingly. After you select the option, you need to upload all the visuals you want to use and add the relevant text. Include a headline and text caption to your ads.

Step Six: Tracking

You will need to edit and constantly optimize your ad campaign on Instagram to generate the best results. There are different tools that you can use to track the performance of your ads on Instagram. The tools that you use will depend on the size of your business and the number of ads you wish to run. Use Power Editor if you want to manage multiple campaigns or if you want precise control over the advertising campaigns. If you are part of a large business team, then use Facebook's Ad Manager. If you are just starting out with Instagram marketing, then use Ads Manager.

Step Six: Tools to Use

The list of social media tools that you can make use of is endless; you might need some help to figure out the best options that are available. Following are some of the most helpful social media tools:

Mention - This can be thought of as the Google alerts for social media. Mention is considered one of the best tools that can help you monitor the presence of your brand on the World Wide Web. Mention also has certain features that let you respond to the mentions that have been made to your brand and to share the news that you might have come across with the industry.

Buffer - This is a really powerful analytical tool that integrates social media publishing in it. Buffer is a helpful social media tool that helps send your updates to the giants of social networking platforms such as LinkedIn, Instagram, Facebook, Twitter, Google+, and many more. This tool comes with an analytic system that is inbuilt and lets you understand the reason why particular posts tend to be working better than the other posts and also the best possible time for making any particular publication based upon the requirements of your audience. Not just this, it also lets you collaborate with your team and keep the account updated with fresh content regularly.

Feedly- Feedly is a content discovery tool. You won't just find good content, you can also share your findings with your audience without trouble. You get to subscribe to the RSS feeds to help keep in tune with all the recent updates on the industry blogs as well as news sites. If you are interested in a topic, then Feedly can be made use of for tracking related content.

Zapier - This is a platform that acts as a connector for all the various services that you make use of individually and lets you synchronize them all to make your work simpler. For instance, if your team usually makes use of HipChat for keeping in touch then by making use of Zapier you will be able to set up the option for automatic notifications within HipChat rooms for any new updates. You will be able to connect all the various apps that you are making use of. If all your apps are integrated on a common platform then your work gets much simpler.

Bottlenose - Bottlenose now comes with a new feature that has a real-time search engine that consolidates all the information from social networking sites and various groups and displays the resultant information in an order or algorithmic importance. The result of all this work is a stream of content that has already been marked from most to least important. When you have information that is already arranged according to your needs, your work gets simpler. You can also share any of the search results. You can also integrate Buffer and Bottlenose for adding any additional content and resources that can be utilized on a later date, if you don't want to overwhelm your followers.

Quintly - This is a really powerful tool that can be made use of for obtaining detailed analytics of social media and helps you keep a track of your business on social media platforms such as Facebook, Twitter, YouTube, Google+, LinkedIn and Instagram as well. Quintly also helps you to benchmark those features that help you compare your performance with those of your competitors in the industry and also against the industry averages. The Quintly dashboard also provides for customization so that you can simply focus on the stats that matter more to you when compared to the rest.

Use these different apps to track your performance on Instagram.

Instagram

Chapter 11 Understanding Analytics

Analytics are the most powerful tools at your disposal. These numbers dictate everything about you - from your potential to partner with brands, to your action plan during content strategy planning. Understanding analytics means digging deep into the world of marketing and getting involved in the nitty-gritty of it all. This is the only place where those with degrees have the advantage. Getting involved with analytics is part of their training, and they are very good at doing so.

Not having a degree does not take away your ability to become masterful on the subject, however. Anybody is capable of anything, especially when they have the tools to do so. I am going to go over some ways now that analytics can help shape your plans and activities.

• Posting Schedule: Targeting times of the day can be a pain. It is, however, absolutely necessary. You need to know when your followers are active so you hit as many as possible. Using the times provided by your analytics, you can easily pinpoint the best times to post content and schedule posts accordingly. This is why scheduling is important - even if you are awake or away from your phone, the show keeps moving on.

• Advertisements: Making sure your money is spent wisely could be the most important thing when you are starting out, whether as a business or as an aspiring influencer. Your analytics determine every aspect of the advertisement, whether it be location or demographic.

• Content Creation: Great analytics means you should make more of that style of post. You can check the analytics on individual posts, and Instagram's analytic suite also shows you which ones have the highest reach and are the best performing. This allows you to move in the right direction according to what your followers interact with the most.

• Contest Guidelines: Depending on who your audience is, you want to tailor contest guidelines to them. Different demographics are willing to put different amounts of time into entering a campaign of any kind. There is a lot that analytics help determine in regard to your campaigns.

There is far more than that, but I will not dilly-dally on the small details. There is far more to talk about than just those!

You need to know where to access those analytics too. There are three websites I am going to mention... two of which I already have mentioned to you. However, this is where I can tell you more about that specific feature, so you really start to get a handle on the different aspects of what these platforms provide.

The main three I love are Hootsuite, Phlanx, and the in-house Instagram analytics suite.

I will provide the reasons below.

• Hootsuite: If I did not say it before, I will say it again; Hootsuite is the master of all things social media. The reason that it is used so widely is the absolute control it gives you over every aspect of your Instagram account. You have the full suite of every analytic you could ever want, and all the data points to match. This gives you a lot of power in making sure you are planning posts and curating content accordingly.

Hootsuite can also run ads for you. This is one of the best ways to do it, since it can also run ads on Facebook and other websites at the same time. In fact, it can even run Google Ads for you. It is just a powerhouse of marketing prowess!

• Phlanx: This is also a great place to pull overall analytic reports from. For some of the features, such as the engagement rate calculators, you do not even need an account. It allows you up to three free searches a day. This is enough to pull your engagement report every day. It helps you to keep track of it.

It is simple at the most basic level. However, everybody needs to start somewhere. For those of you who cannot pay for a full service analytics program, this is a great place to start. It will not give you everything you need. But, when used in conjunction with the next item on this list, it is powerful indeed.

• Instagram Analytics Suite: Yes, the in-house analytics made it into the list. I have found their numbers to be pretty well rounded in terms of usability. They give you a great idea of what posts are performing well, which ones are flopping, when your fans are online, etc. It even gives you full analytics to your stories, which is a huge plus.

These will serve you well. After all, I would not talk about them so in-depth if they were not truly the best tools for the job. You can teach yourself all about analytics just by studying them and checking them daily. Getting a feel for the rhythm and what your account looks like in terms of analytics is important.

So, about your engagement rate. This analytic is especially important for aspiring influencers, and less so for businesses. Influencers need to know how well they are doing in terms of their fanbase. This determines when you should launch merch, or even a website, or do anything in terms of promoting yourself. It can also tell you when a good time to start up a contest would be.

Engagement rates will also determine when you should feel comfortable reaching out to companies or brands in terms of sponsorship deals, or even giveaways you may run together. Remember, they have those analytics and they will absolutely use them.

There are a few different ways you can increase your engagement rate. I will set some out below.

• Engage with other similar accounts. You need to engage every day. I cannot stress this point enough. The only way to get people to interact with you is to interact with them. It is a group effort and you need to constantly be in contact with other accounts to be successful.

This is especially true for influencers and brands. Make sure you have notifications on for their accounts, following the 10% rule for your allotted amount of followed accounts. Making sure that at least half of those accounts are influencers and brands is a great way to see them in your feed and be able to interact on a daily basis.

Also, make sure you flip through people's stories and interact with them. Answer polls, questions, quizzes, and whatever else they might have up.

• Use strategic hashtags. Carefully choose what you use. You need to make sure that you are using hashtags to the best of your ability.

Check the posts of successful accounts and see what they are using for their hashtags. Combined with this, look to see how many people are following the tag and make sure to do the half-and-half trick. To refresh you, make sure half the tags have a following of less than 100k. The other half are fair game for any number and should be more "generic" in nature.

• Put effort into your captions. Longer captions engage your audience. It makes them read more about you and become more involved in your life. You should really put effort into your captions by using tools that allow you to add spacing into them. You can even find online tools which will allow you to make text bold or italicized. The internet is truly a wonderful place!

• Add a QOTD to your posts. To get people talking to you, make sure to add a Question of the Day to your posts. This is a call to action where you are compelling people to answer your question. Make sure most of them are pretty simple; most people are going to want to give a one-word answer.

For example, asking if they prefer one thing to another is a good strategy. Or, ask them what their favorite song is. Anything goes!

• Use all the features in your story. You have an array of different tools you can use here. There are lots of cool stickers, effects, engagement boosting tools, and more. You can even put music in your story! Posting up polls, quizzes, and more get people interacting on your story... and perhaps clicking over to your profile if they are intrigued.

Boosting your engagement goes beyond even these strategies, however. A lot of it is integrated into the other things you are doing on your Instagram account.

Much like the analytics driving everything, engagement is a result of those analytics and should be nurtured even beyond this.

You need to figure out when the best times to post for you are. Looking at your analytics on Instagram, you can easily see when people are awake and using Instagram actively. These are the times when you need to schedule things to post for you. If you are posting when they are asleep, they are not going to see what you are posting. It will not be relevant or show up in their feed. The algorithm on Instagram is constantly changing and understanding analytics has never been more important as a result.

Posting should be done when people are most awake, which will vary during the week. If you are going to be posting three times a week, make sure that you schedule your posts for the busiest times during the three busiest days. These days will most likely remain fairly constant, and most people find that it is the weekend where activity shoots up. For this reason, I generally suggest posting something on Monday, Wednesday, and Saturday. This gives you a full range of days with a different pull. Making a themed QOTD or story post alongside it will also boost engagement.

Furthermore, understanding your audience becomes crucial. Knowing their patterns of activity is great, but you need to know more. There are definitely better analytics out there if you are using another program to keep track of them. Knowing who your audience is allows you to better cater to them. There is a huge difference between a teenage girl, for example, and a mother of three. Understanding these differences and the habits of your audience allows you to market directly to them. This is beyond necessary if you hope to see profit on your investments.

Again, three posts per day is the maximum you should be posting. This may be impossible for you, depending on how much content you have backed up and how much time you can put into cultivating or curating more of it. This is why featuring other accounts' posts can be useful, too, since this is content curation rather than content creation.

I will explain these two terms below:

• Content Creation: Whenever you create something to be posted to your Instagram account, this is content creation. It is your personal work that you have made to post onto your account. It is entirely yours.

• Content Curation: This is the act of taking content from other creators, posting it on your platform, and fully crediting them. This means tagging them in the photo, as well as talking about them in the description. It is a great way to say "Hey, this is really cool and I love it". Most people do not mind having posts featured so long as they are tagged and fully credited. Hootsuite has a feature that will cultivate things automatically for your convenience.

Now that you understand the two, more and more of this will make sense. Learning industry terms is important for making people understand that you are literate in the art of social media. Professionalism goes a long way in cultivating a strong public image with close networking ties.

Now that we have all of the above out of the way, I think we should talk about the elephant in the room. We are all too aware that you can purchase followers. This is something that many businesses or accounts do in order to boost their follower count and gain more legitimacy. As people are learning about it, they are also learning what constitutes a "fake" follower, and how to see an account filled with them.

Some of the signs that an account is fake are as follows:

• A dead giveaway is that they are following thousands of accounts. This is especially true if they are inactive and almost nobody is following them back.

• Their usernames are garbled nonsense. Normally, people put at least some thought into their usernames. Numbers and letters, or strange spellings, are also a sign that an account is fake.

• They have few posts, and the ones up are nonsense. Having the same photo over and over again, or very few posts that have no caption, shows they are most likely a fake account

There is a way to stop them, however. When you find fake accounts, report them immediately as spam. Make sure that you check who is following you as much as you can and report fake followers as you find them. Fake accounts also screw up your engagement rates. Beware of them!

Besides fake followers, there is also automation at work. Most people do not realize that these are such a hot commodity, but the truth is that a lot of people use them. However, it is important to note that they are very much against the Terms of Service for Instagram. If you are found to be using one, you can say good-bye to your account.

There are a few other dangers you can associate with automation too. Being "shadow banned" is a real threat. Essentially, the Instagram algorithm will see that you are making a ton of comments at once. It will flag you as a potential spam account and you will be banned from commenting on or liking other posts - even your own! This is obviously something you want to avoid.

On that note, do not copy and paste comments onto a bunch of photos. This is so disingenuous and really makes you look awful if people catch onto it. Remember, real growth is slow at first and you have to build a great public image to have real success.

Automating programs work pretty easily. They will go through and do the following things:

- Follow accounts for you

- Leave comments on photos

- Like as many posts as you set them to

These are all great features, right? Wrong. The only thing an Automator is going to do is get you banned from Instagram. Although some people use them, I never suggest this route. The chance of getting caught is too great, even if it is small. It also removes your ability to comment sincerely on other people's posts. That is the way you want to go about it.

The benefits of automators are as follows:

- Reach a bunch of accounts at once.

- Interaction with other accounts skyrockets.

- You can gain followers more quickly.

The dangers, however? They far outweigh these benefits:

- You could very well get banned. Violating the ToS of any website is a bad look. This puts you in danger of losing everything you have been working for. For influencers and businesses, this is simply not worth the risk. You need to make sure that real growth is happening, but a fake boost will only hurt you in the long run. The money maker is your connection to and influence on your fans. You need to make a genuine effort in connecting with them.

• Even if you do not get banned, you may face a temporary block. Being shadow banned enough times is enough to get you permanently banned. Also, it disables your ability to interact for at least an hour or so. This is a huge blow to your ability to get scheduled posts up and keep updated on what is happening.

• The comments are not genuine and might make people angry. Some people even go as far as to block accounts which are leaving obviously automated comments on their posts. People absolutely hate it - it is selfish, and really quite rude.

I think that I need not say more on this topic. Obviously, using an automator is just all around a bad idea. I do not suggest it. In fact, I suggest that you steer clear of them as a whole.

Chapter 12 How Does the Instagram Algorithm Work?

The algorithm is a deciding factor of who views your published content and who doesn't. This applies to both SEO and social media. However, these algorithms tend to change frequently, which makes a strategy that was effective before becoming obsolete. For this reason, you need to continuously advance as well.

When it comes to Instagram, especially, posting frequently using the appropriate hashtags won't imply that your content will get to the relevant audience. Rather, you will have to reflect on how to work around the algorithm to diversify your approach to marketing on Instagram. In essence, the value of the algorithm is something you can't underrate, which is what makes it something vital to consider. In this chapter, you will learn the way the Instagram algorithm works and how you can work around it to achieve the best results. Now that you understand what the algorithm is, how exactly does the Instagram algorithm function?

How Does the Instagram Algorithm Function?

The new Instagram algorithm determines the arrangement of the posts that will be viewed by users when they scroll through their feed. Using certain signals, it gives priority to posts, pushing those that are relevant to the top and offering them a high level of visibility, while the less relevant content is moved to the lower end of the user's feed.

Instagram published some information in June 2018, showing a few elements that the algorithm capitalizes on when ranking the content on the feed of users. Although it is vital to understand that the recent algorithm could be altered later in the future, there are still some major factors used to rank a post which you need to consider in your Instagram strategy. They include:

• Connection with the user: If a specific user has engaged with a host of your previous content, they have a higher probability of seeing your recent content. This allows for repeat and continuous engagement on your content, which is vital for the development of loyal followers.

• Level of interest shown by the user: This signal is dependent on if the user engages with other accounts and posts similar to yours when they go through Instagram. In essence, any user who shows interest in content related to yours, has a higher tendency to see posts you make.

• How recent the post was: Previously, Instagram utilized a sequential feed. However, this is no longer the case, but that does not mean the timing is not a factor to date. Posts which were recently uploaded will be pushed above the feed, while less recent posts will come up further below.

Instagram also shared some additional considerations which are vital; they include:

• If users follow numerous accounts, your struggle to get to the top of their feed will be more

• If you are not on the top of the feeds of users who don't stay so long on Instagram or check out the application, the chances of your content been seen are lower.

- In comparison to Instagram business accounts, personal accounts are not instantly at a disadvantage when it has to do with organic reach.

Now that you understand how the Instagram algorithm works, you need to learn how you can alter your strategy to get to more of your clients. To do this, the steps below may be of help:

Don't Focus On Reach Alone, Relationships Matter Too

Loyalty from your audience alongside continuous interaction from those who follow you, now has a higher level of importance, since it will be able to provide you with a spot at the top of their feeds.

There are ways to establish these relationships using your content, some of which include:

- Reminders that urge users to share their opinions and things they feel and offer you a chance to begin a discussion with them.

- Uploading posts that help build engagement, like Instagram contests or tag-a-friend post that urge users to leave comments.

- User-generated content concerning your brands that have been posted by your followers. In addition to aspiring more UGC, users might tag you in the posts they make and further develop your Instagram presence.

However, if you want to make headway on Instagram, you need to think beyond your posts.

Leave Comments On Posts from Brands and Users Relevant to You

You can also interact with the people on their posts to develop relationships beyond your posts, by making relevant and engaging comments on content from influencers pertinent to you, prospective clients, and related organizations.

Also, leaving posts on more established accounts that have a huge following can provide more visibility to your profile and comment as well. Take a look at accounts that the audience you are targeting has a probability to follow, follow these accounts, and become a part of the conversation. If you decide to go through this route, be authentic, and ensure you make relevant comments. Don't just leave non-specific responses or sales pitches. Show the personality of your brand and engage in a relevant manner.

You can take it a step further by turning on post notifications for certain accounts. This will ensure you can leave comments promptly, enhancing the possibility that it will get visibility, thanks to the focus of Instagram feeds on recent posts. To achieve this, it is essential that you are a follower of the account. Tap the three dots at the right-hand angle of the application and hit "Turn on post notifications" to begin getting push notifications the instant they upload a new post.

Upload Posts During Peak Periods

Since the recency of posts is still a major consideration for where your posts will be placed in the feeds of your followers, you need to exploit it. It, not a bad idea to get a huge level of engagement when your post first goes live, and it will inform Instagram that this a post that would love to be seen by a higher number of your followers.

To enhance the possibility of each post you make, make efforts to upload content when your followers are most active.

Leave Responses to Comments When They Are New

When you leave responses to as many comments as you can, you will enhance your number of comments while boosting further replies. Additionally, it increases your probabilities of getting more engagement while the potential reach of your post is at its highest.

When you respond to comments, it can lead to additional comments from the main poster. Even something as simple as a thank-you can go a long way. However, in some circumstances, you can begin conversations which give you substantial engagement that will aid in increasing the reach of your posts and other posts in the future.

Use Community Hashtags to Get to Users Who Are Active

Instagram hashtags can aid in increasing your reach by ensuring you come up in significant searches. However, if you want this approach to be efficient, you have to pick hashtags that your audience uses in searching for content as well as other users.

Community hashtags, in particular, are quite active. Although they may not have as many posts as the other well-known hashtags, they are already being shared and explored by numerous groups on Instagram who are in search of ways to create connections with others that have an interest in that movement, topic or community.

From here, you will obtain views that can provide you with clicks via your engagement, profile, and prospective followers. Although these relevant hashtags will differ according to industry, it is easy to find them because they define your perfect customer and are constantly filled with new posts related to your niche.

Repost Already Existing Content to Add a New Feel

If you have issues generating adequate content on Instagram to get more pull in terms of traffic, or you want to ensure that particular content gets seen by as many users as possible, a great way to go is to repurpose previous content, especially as your follower base increases.

This will push you leading content to the top feed once more. In addition, those who missed it when you initially posted it will get to enjoy it this time. Although many brands just delete an old post and post it how they previously shared it, repurposing content works differently.

If you have no idea of how to properly repurpose content, the methods below can help:

- Include a caption different from the one you used previously

- Make a video of the past post images

- Integrate new designs into the picture. You can easily do this if you edit the image of the previous post using the various filters available to you on Instagram.

- Use popular hashtags to share your existing content once more like #throwbackthursday

It can save you a lot of time if you repurpose content. However, you should not rely on it. Remember to diversify, and go through your feed to get rid of duplicate content. Users will still have the capacity to check your previous posts, and you want to make sure they don't come across the same image numerous times.

Utilize Stories to Gain Attention

A lot of marketers focus on Instagram stories because the algorithm they use is not the same as the ones used in the posts on your feed. It is also an amazing method of interacting with your followers and enhancing loyalty. This leads to an increase in engagement on your stagnant posts, which in turn leads to additional reach.

The following are ways to do this:

•   Incorporate hashtag stickers to your branded hashtag

•   Encourage engagement using interactive stickers

•   Share Stories uploaded by other users

•   Urge you, users, to put on post notifications

When you do this in the right manner, like subtly sending a reminder to users, it can prove to the algorithm how significant your brand is to your community. Those who turn their notifications on, in addition to seeing more of your content, will have more likelihood of engaging with your posts.

Make Sure Your Posts Are Amazing

Instagram has made it known numerous times that producing amazing content is the only method of increasing the feed ranking of your content. However, Instagram's major appeal has always been the unstated rule that you need high-quality pictures.

So if you want better engagement, this might mean you need to take a different approach. You can get the services of an experienced photographer and find out what you can learn. You can also download new tools that can increase your knowledge of editing photos.

Remember to Develop Relationships

If you want the best Instagram has to offer, you need to do more than regularly post content. Rather, it is vital that you also pay attention to developing a relationship while keeping communication with users on your pot and beyond them.

Social media algorithms tend to change. However, if you take the innovative and change with them, you will learn that there are numerous methods of getting the audience you desire.

Chapter 13 How to Make Storytelling More Compelling by Knowing Your Audience

Now that you have created your Instagram page and have also started communicating with your followers on Instagram, the next thing you need to focus on is to come up with ways in which you can reach a wider audience. Essentially, it is all about understanding how you can create a huge fan base for yourself without being someone famous outside the Instagram community.

If you use Instagram for marketing, then you might have noticed a dip in the number of followers you have at some point or the other. Don't worry about this. It might happen that you aren't receiving as many likes, comments or new followers like you did in the past. In any case, it isn't just you who hits a snag like this. In this section, you will learn about different ways in which you can become a compelling storyteller and increase your reach. In this section, you will learn about the ways in which you can become a better storyteller by understanding your audience.

Select A Theme

You need to select a theme for your Instagram page that will appeal to your niche. It is not just about selecting a theme, but you need to stick to it as well.

What's even better is that if you can make a unique name for yourself. If you want users on Instagram to follow you, then you need to publish consistent and high-quality content frequently. If they know that they can count on your page for this, they will want to follow you.

Join Instagram Engagement Groups

Are you trying to figure out how to increase your followers on Instagram? If yes, then you need to join Instagram engagement groups. It might be difficult to make your way into the biggest Instagram engagement groups, you will certainly get a list of more targeted Instagram followers by sticking to your niche. It is quite easy to find Instagram engagement groups. If you are a member of such a group, then it is quite easy to obtain followers and receive likes from those who have similar interests to you. If you are serious about increasing your visibility, then ensure that you return the favor and follow the fan pages for people who join the group.

Even if it may not help with immediate sales, it helps your brand gain goodwill. You need to understand that this strategy will work only in the short-term and is not effective in the long run.

Ask Customers to Share their Photos

You can always ask your customers to share their photos in your feed. In fact, it is a good strategy that you can use if you are just starting out with Instagram marketing. It also goes a long way in establishing social proof for your brand. If you haven't been doing great business, then reach out to your target audience and offer a free gift or any other incentive if they share quality images of the products you sell. Obviously, giving incentives is not a long-term strategy, but it certainly works for increasing short-term sales. It helps you grow as a brand. As more and more users start to see the content shared by customers, it naturally increases the interest in your brand.

Produce Content Your Audience Will Love

Whenever you are thinking about the type of content that is ideal for your business, you need to focus on ensuring that the posts are extraordinary. You need to create content that your audience will love. It isn't about you; it is about your audience. It might seem obvious, but content creation is one aspect of Instagram that a lot of people seem to neglect. You need to understand what your audience likes and you need to create content accordingly.

Regardless of what you decide to use, you need to be able to connect with your audience. When creating content, keep this age-old adage "beauty lies in the eyes of the beholder" in your mind. This is the reason why you need to establish a good relationship with your audience so that you can learn about the type of content that will appeal to them. There have been numerous occasions where people decided to post something that they thought their audience would like, but to their utter dismay, it turned out to be a dud.

One way in which you can produce great content is to check out the kind of content that your competition is posting. You also need to take a note of the imagery that they use. Also, never just copy and paste stuff.

Choosing the Right Instagram Content

If you want a huge following on Instagram, then you need to produce high-quality content. It must not only be tailor-made for your Instagram page, but must also be exactly what your target audience needs. When you are creating content, you need to find the right approach as well as the style. It is important because your content will be the way that your followers will recognize your business.

Negotiate to get Shoutouts

You will also want to know about the different ways in which you can obtain a greater number of followers. One of the simplest ways to do this is via shoutouts. If you decide to use this trend, then your page will gain a lot of popularity within a couple of weeks or even months.

Essentially, shoutouts are a form of advertising other pages, and are usually done by authority pages or influencers. Speaking in a general sense, a shoutout is when a famous Instagrammer or influencer mentions your page on their own account and then tells their followers to check your page and encourages them to follow you. Shoutout is a great way to get your name in front of a huge audience of potential followers.

Use Apps to Increase Instagram Followers

There are different apps that you can use to increase your Instagram followers. A lot of people tend to use a bot to achieve this purpose. In most cases, they are known as Instagress. It works quite well, at least initially, and allows users to gain their first couple of thousands of Instagram followers. Eventually, the popular handles stop using the bots since they aren't of any use after gaining the necessary following. Unfortunately, Instagress and other similar apps that are used to increase the number of followers are usually shut down after they are noticed by the administrators of the platform. It might seem tempting to use something like this, but it is better if you avoid it.

Repost Other's Content

There are some who entirely build their Instagram profiles based on reposting the content created by others. The only way in which you can successfully do this is by giving the necessary credit to the creator and by obtaining their permission before you go ahead and post their content. In fact, it is one of the policies of Instagram that you need to seek the permission of that specific content's creator before you use it.

Use Insights

It's quite easy to track your followers and post's impressions you receive on Instagram. One thing that you need to keep in mind if you want to gain more followers is to convert your Instagram page into a business page. Once you do this, you can use the information available on Insights to monitor the way your posts are doing. Not just this, there are several other metrics that you can monitor as well.

Chapter 14 Tools, Links and Resources on how to win with Instagram

Instagram tools are becoming a huge hit online, and it seems like more and more tools are being rolled out all the time. Instagram has a variety of tools, all of which serve a different purpose, but each just as useful as the next at helping you put your best marketing efforts forward. The social media world is a competitive one, and Instagram has proved itself to be a strong contender, continuously coming up with more ways and tools to improve and adapt to the ever-changing world of marketing and advertising. Let's take a look at some of the various tools available and what they're used for.

Best Instagram Scheduling Tools

Here's a list of some of the best tools which can be used for scheduling content on Instagram:

Buffer

In terms of managing social network accounts, Buffer is an absolute timesaver. It allows you to schedule and publish posts on many online platforms like Twitter, Pinterest, and Facebook. It also provides thorough analytics for your online campaigns. Buffer is also available on Instagram. So it gives business owners the flexibility of scheduling posts on Instagram.

Buffer's simplicity in terms of usage is perhaps the most significant thing about it. So, users need not worry about a learning curve or following tutorials. Using Buffer is as simple as these three steps: hooking up your business accounts, scheduling your content, and you are all set.

Buffer allows you to schedule up to a maximum of 10 posts for free, after which you're asked to upgrade to any of their plans for more posting options. Their plans are budget-friendly and go as low as $10 per month. This plan covers up to 10 social media profiles and a hundred scheduled posts.

This one is perfect for scheduling content, and it comes with both a free and pro version (which is paid for). This tool allows users to schedule single-image posts right from their desktops or mobile apps, conveniently allowing you to schedule ahead of time.

Sendible

Sendible can be used to schedule posts, create reports on analytics, collaborate with your entire team, or even reply to the comments of your followers using a social network inbox. It works great for agencies too. You can also use Sendible to make your motivational quote or Instagram image utilizing their canvas integration. Your videos can also be published directly to your Instagram account from Sendible. The app provides different packages, but their micro package allows up to four social network accounts at $24 per month. They bill annually.

Hootsuite

Hootsuite is a very recognized platform for social media management. You can integrate it with all the core social networks apart from Instagram. With this application, you can automate posts and send reminders for posts. It is not as expensive as the competition, and you can use it as an iOS, Android, or web application.

Even if you develop the best content, posting it at the wrong time may not get you the traffic you want. You need to learn the right posting time for your content.

Hooper

A great tool for helping you schedule and manage your statistics. This tool is exclusively for Instagram scheduling only, and besides the convenience of scheduling, users can get phone previews to see how their post looks on a mobile device before approving it, content calendars, and even a space for you to save your draft content if there are posts which you want to come back later on and tweak.

Later

The name is a dead giveaway with this one. Later is a scheduling tool, and according to eCommerce Facebook group members, it is one of the most popular Instagram scheduling tools out there. The most notable thing about this tool is its easy scheduler and visual calendar. On top of that, it comes with a link.bio feature, which turns your bio links into -voila! - shoppable URLs. Just what the doctor ordered to peak those sales numbers. Later is a robust post-scheduling Instagram tool. According to the website, they are the go-to company for over 600,000 top brands, influencers, and agencies. It is indeed one of the most popular scheduling tools in the world, serving many entrepreneurs, small companies, and bloggers.

Later also allows you to manage comments on your Instagram. It offers a free plan and a premium plan. On the free plan, users are allowed to schedule not more than 30 posts (only photo posts) per month for a single social profile. Going up to $49 per month from $9 per month, the paid plans support up to a maximum of 5 profiles and unlimited posts.

Schedugram

This tool is perfect for scheduling all types of posts, although it is one of the pricier tools compared to a lot of the other ones. Schedugram comes with features which include content creation, a feature which is explicitly designed for Instagram. Its built-in photo editing, location, shopping, drag and drop calendar function, mention, carousel ad options, videos, and stories are only a peek into what this tool is capable of.

Tools for Content Creation on Instagram

Here's a list of some of the tools you might find useful for your content creation efforts:

Boomerang

If you love those quirky, funny, short video loops you've become so accustomed to on Instagram, Boomerang is how it's done. It is now a built-in part of Instagram's story features, and it is absolutely perfect for creating on-the-go short video loops anytime, anywhere.

Canva

This tool comes with both free and paid templates for you to choose from to help you create your best content yet. From email headers to Instagram posts, Canva will leave you spoilt for choice when it comes to which templates to use for your Instagram profile. You can even choose to upload your finished products directly onto your Instagram account once you're happy with it.

Kapwing

If videos and memes are your choices of entertainment, this is the tool you're going to want to use to create them. Specializing in video editing and creation, this free online content-creation tool lets you create memes quickly and efficiently, add music to your texts, resize and trim your videos, create slow-motion content, add subtitles, and more. You'll enjoy browsing through its many features.

PicFlow

This tool is provided free, although it comes with in-app purchases if you need more advanced features at your disposal. PicFlow is a good choice when it comes to turning your photos into a video slideshow, and you can even add on some music to make it a little bit more interesting. PicFlow does come with a watermark though, and you're going to have to pay to get upgraded to have those watermarks removed.

Repost

For sharing and curating content, Repost is going to be your go-to. With this tool, your favorite videos and photos on Instagram can quickly and easily be reposted (don't forget to give credit to the original owner of the content though if you're reposting anything from a follower or influencer). Reposting can be a big help to your marketing efforts, especially when it comes to encouraging user-generated content. Plus, it's free!

VSCO

A tool that's used for editing your videos and your photos. This one is ideal for all those marketers looking to create some really striking content and visuals for their profiles. VSCO has some pretty powerful video and image-editing features, and when done right, your visuals can look almost as though they were shot professionally. For the more serious content creators, there are preset options available which can be used with other tools like Photoshop and Lightroom.

Tools for Managing Multiple Channels

Managing multiple social media platforms can be challenging and time-consuming, which is why these multi-channel tools can come in handy during these moments:

CrowdFire

With both free and paid options available, this social media account management tool is perfect for the busy marketer who's got a lot on their plate. Run on a web-based platform, this "everything under one roof" social media management tool lets you control your blog content, schedule, publish, curate, and even track your social media mentions all through this one, seamless tool. If you're looking to monitor your post analytics and social media accounts (not just Instagram), CrowdFire can do that for you too.

Sendible

Another multi-channel tool to make life a little more efficient for you is Sendible. The only catch with this one is that it can be a little on the pricier side. This is because it is designed mostly for agencies. Small business owners and those who are just starting out might find the added monthly cost with this one a pinch on the budget, but it does come with some really great, robust features. This tool has got Canva integration, plus team collaborations features, CRM, and account and social media management which make scheduling and managing your Instagram account a breeze if you're willing to spend on it.

Status Rew

A tool that is perfect if you've got 10 social media profiles, 10 Twitter sources, 2000 scheduled posts per profile, and three members running the show. Status Rew has even got social listening features, which generally means you can sync your social engagement to the platform, draft replies, monitor keywords, and even moderate comments without ever having to switch back and forth between Instagram and this tool.

Instagram Influencer Locating Tools

Influencers are everywhere on social media, and sooner or later, you're going to need to work with them, at least once. So why not get on board with some tools that could help you locate the best influencers that your business might consider collaborating with?

UserGems

A tool that is perfect for helping you locate both influencers and even micro-influencers. The best part? These could be among your very own existing customer base! This tool uses real-time customer intelligence and data from your customers to help you detect the best influencers who are popular among your niche market.

FameBit

A handy tool which lets you connect directly with influencers who are on the lookout for new campaign opportunities. Once you've set up your campaign type on this tool (narrowing down your factors and budget), you'll be able to get to work quickly connecting with influencers who are going to be the right fit for what you need.

Best Tools for Instagram Hashtag Researching

Hashtags are as much a part of the Instagram world as having visuals are. Without a hashtag, your post might look almost naked and incomplete on your profile. That's how much users have become accustomed to seeing hashtags on this social media site. To make your hashtag research a little bit easier, use the following tools to help you out:

Autohash

A tool which is offered free but with in-app purchases for additional features. This is an Android-based app though, and it will help you locate the relevant hashtags on Instagram for your business. Using artificial intelligence technology, Autohash will review the images on your profile, detect the objects within that image, and then proceed to suggest which hashtags might be the most relevant to your content. You also have the option of adding some of the popular hashtags to your clipboard to be used later on.

Display Purposes

Another free tool which helps you locate the perfect hashtag(s) for your profile. This web-based platform works by helping you out with the research portion of it and provides you with the relevant hashtags for your profile content. Simply start by keying in a keyword or a hashtag, and Display Purposes will suggest even more hashtags for you to choose from.

Focal Mark

Another tool which comes for free, but has in-app purchases which means you might have to be willing to spend on certain features. This one works well on both Android and iOS, and it helps you out by choosing which hashtags are going to work best for your profile. Focal Mark works by using an algorithm which takes the photo's subject, location, and the camera which was used to capture that content. It then helps you detect the most popular hashtags which would be the most relevant to your content.

TopTager

Who doesn't love free tools? Marketers will love this one because not only does it display all the most popular and trending hashtags in real time, it also helps you find the hashtags which will be the best match for your keywords. TopTager uses the copy-and-paste function, a simple solution for you to quickly cut and paste the popular hashtags you want to use and put them on your posts.

Instagram Linking Tools

Want to create an effective link on your bio? You can with these tools:

LinkTree

The perfect tool for all your bio linking strategy needs. Why? Because it helps you manage the bio link on your Instagram for you. If you've worked with Instagram for a while, you'll know that you can only put one link on your bio at any given time. Therefore, whenever you want to change it depending on the promotions, special deals, or blog posts which are trending at the moment for your business, it can be a rather cumbersome process to keep manually changing it. Enter LinkTree, to solve all your problems. This tool works by providing your audience with a link which leads them directly to a landing page, where they will find different sections they can click on.

Soldsie

This tool is pretty steep cost-wise because the price would depend on the number of clicks which your link gets. Soldsie caters more towards publications and online retail stores.

Photo-Editing Tools You Need

This is probably among the most important and essential tools you need since Instagram relies heavily on visuals. Here are some of the best photo-editing tools out there for Instagram to give your profile that extra oomph:

Afterlight 2

An all-in-one tool for all your photo editing needs, Afterlight 2 can quickly become a favorite because of all the filters, frames, and typography options that it presents you with. The array of choices help you pick the best ones that will make an impact on your images. You even have the option of creating your own filters with this one!

Enlight

Looking to turn your visuals into the work of art that it is? Enlight will help you out with this one.

Facetune

For the images that need a little help and touching up, Facetune is here to save the day. If you're not keen on fancy editing programs like Photoshop, this one might do the trick, although it is more suitable for photos with apparel products.

Photoshop Express

A longtime favorite, Photoshop Express has a wide array of features to help take your images one step further. Anything from cropping, text tools, exposure corrections, perspective corrections, blemish removal, filters and border additions, this tool is here to satisfy all your photo editing needs. And for free, too.

Chapter 15 Different Ways to Make Money on Instagram

One of the neat things about Instagram is that there are a lot of different ways that you can earn money through this platform. While this guidebook has spent a lot of time talking about how businesses can grow their following and earn customers, the same tips can be used for individuals who are looking to earn money online. A business may decide to just sell their own products online to customers and make a profit that way, but there are other methods that small businesses (depending on who they are) and individuals can use to earn a very nice income online from all the hard work they have done to gain followers and a good reputation on this platform. Let's take a look at some of the different ways that you can potentially make money on Instagram.

Affiliate Marketing

The first option is to work as an affiliate marketer. Basically, with this option, you are going to promote a product for a company and then get paid for each sale.

This is something that is really popular with bloggers because they work on getting their website set up, and then they can write articles about a product, or sell advertising space, and then they make money on any sales through their links. You can do the same thing with Instagram as well.

When you want to work with affiliate marketing with Instagram, you need to post attractive images of the products you choose and try to drive sales through the affiliate URL. You will get this affiliate link through the company you choose to advertise with. Just make sure that you are going with an affiliate that offers high-quality products so you don't send your followers substandard products. And check that you will actually earn a decent commission on each one.

Once you get your affiliate URL, add it to the captions of the posts you are promoting or even in the bio if you plan to stick with this affiliate for some time. It is also possible to use the bitly extension to help shorten the address or you can customize your affiliate link. It is also possible for you to hook up the Instagram profile and blog so that when people decide to purchase through the link at all, you will get the sale.

If you have a good following on Instagram already, then this method of making money can be pretty easy. You just need to find a product that goes with the theme of your page and then advertise it to your customers. Make sure that the product is high-quality so that your customers are happy with the recommendations that you give.

Create a Sponsored Post

Instagram users that have a following that is pretty engaged have the ability to earn some money through the platform simply by creating sponsored content that is original and that various brands can use. To keep it simple, a piece of sponsored product through Instagram could be a video or a picture that is going to highlight a brand/specific product. Include branded hashtags, @mentions and links in the posts.

While most brands don't really need a formal brand ambassadorship for the creators of this kind of content, it is pretty common for some of these brands to find certain influencers to help them come up with new content over and over again. However, you must make sure that the brands and the products that you use are a good fit for the image that you worked so hard to create on Instagram. Show followers how this brand is already fitting into your lifestyle so they can implement it as well.

Sell Pictures

This one is one that may seem obvious, but it can be a great way for photographers to showcase some of the work that you do. If you are an amateur or professional photographer, you will find that Instagram is the perfect way to advertise and even sell your shots. You can choose to sell your services to big agencies or even to individuals who may need the pictures for their websites or other needs.

If you are posting some of the pictures that you want to sell on your profile, make sure that each of them has a watermark on them. This makes it hard for customers to take the pictures without paying you first. You can also use captions to help list out the details of selling those pictures so there isn't any confusion coming up with it at all.

To make this one work, take the time to keep your presence on Instagram active. This ensures that the right people and the right accounts are following. This is also a good place to put in the right hashtags so that people are able to find your shots. You may even want to take the time to get some engagement and conversations started with big agencies in the photography world who can help you grow even more.

Promote Your Services, Products, or Business

If you already run a business, then Instagram can be a good way to market and promote your business. For example, if you already sell some products, use Instagram to post shots of the products, ones that the customer can't already find on a website. Some other ways that you can promote your business through Instagram include:

• Behind the scenes: These are very popular on Instagram. Show your followers what it takes to make the products you sell. Show them some of your employees working. Show something that the follower usually won't be able to see because it is unique and makes them feel like they are part of your inner circle.

• Pictures from your customers: If you pick out a good hashtag and share it with your customers, they will start to use it with some of their own pictures. You can then use this content to help promote your business even more.

- Exclusive offers and infographics: You can take the time to market your services through Instagram with some exclusive offers and infographics of your products. This works really well if the offers are ones the customer wouldn't be able to find anywhere else.

Sell Advertising Space on Your Page

If you have a large enough following, you may be able to get other brands and companies interested in buying advertising on your profile. They will use this as a way to gain access to your followers in order to increase their own followers, sell a product, or increase their own brand awareness. This is the perfect opportunity for you to make some money from all the hard work that you have done for your own page.

There are many different ways that you can do this. You can offer to let them do a video and then post it as your story, promote a post on your profile, or use any of the other ad options above. You can then charge for the type of space they decide to use, the amount of time they want to advertise for, and how big of an audience you are promoting them in front of.

Become a Brand Ambassador

This is something that is becoming really popular with MLM companies. There is so much competition on Twitter and Facebook that many are turning to use Instagram as a new way to promote their products and get followers that they may not be able to find through other means. And because of the visual aspects of the platform, these ambassadors can really showcase some of the products through pictures and videos.

There are many companies that you can choose from when it comes to being a brand ambassador. Since you have already taken some time to build up your audience and you have a good following, so if you can find a good product to advertise to your followers, you can make a good amount of money. You have to pick out a product that your followers will enjoy, ones that go with the theme of your profile to enhance your potential profits.

As you can see, there are many different options that you can choose from when you want to make some money through your Instagram account. All of the different methods make it perfect no matter what your interests are. After you have some time to build up your own audience and you have quite a few followers already looking at your profile and looking to you for advice, you can leverage this in order to make some money through this social media platform.

Conclusion

Social media is the singular, most powerful tool in reaching out to a large number of people. If you do not make it a part of your marketing strategy, especially if you are a small business venture, then you will find yourself facing a huge loss in the Digital World of Today, where everything runs on hashtagging and commenting on a post.

Instagram is a mobile photography platform where you must make use of pictures to tell your customers who you are, what you sell and why they should try your product. A picture is indeed worth a thousand words – keep them fun, interactive and cool so that your customer base grows day by day. Use all your social media accounts, from Facebook to Tumblr to promote your brand – interact with your customers and analyze the trending tags in the market to examine what they want and plan your business model accordingly.

Remember that the key to making your Instagram activity effective is engagement and reach. As important as gaining followers is, it's as important to maintain them. This can be achieved with quality content and interaction with your followers.

Make sure that you are consistent in updating your profile and keep things interesting, but relevant to your brand.

If you keep all these fundamental tips in mind, you're on track for success on Instagram. Good luck!

Thank you once again for choosing this book and I hope that you found it useful!

Printed in Great Britain
by Amazon

22215950R00106